# Enthusiasm

SWAMI
CHIDVILASANANDA

SWAMI
CHIDVILASANANDA

A SIDDHA YOGA PUBLICATION
PUBLISHED BY SYDA FOUNDATION

*Living in the divine experience of enthusiasm,*
*staying in touch with the divinity that abides within you,*
*letting it sing through all your actions,*
*allowing this great glory to shine forth*
*and lend its radiance to your whole day —*
*this is our theme and this is our goal.*

— Swami Chidvilasananda

Published by SYDA Foundation
371 Brickman Rd., P.O. Box 600, South Fallsburg, New York 12779, USA

*Acknowledgments*
*With dedication and love, many people participated in preparing these talks on enthusiasm for publication. We would like to thank Peggy Bendet, our skilled managing editor; Valerie Ann Sensabaugh, text coordinator; Diane Fast and Laura Turley, copy editors; Cheryl Crawford, designer; Stéphane Dehais, typesetter; Osnat Shurer and Sushila Traverse, production supervisors; Hans Turstig, who gave guidance with Sanskrit; Viju Kulkarni, who identified the* bhajans*; and all the others who offered their service in the spirit of the book's message and meaning. We thank each one for a unique and inspiring contribution.*

*Kshama Ferrar and Sarah Scott*



Printed in the United States of America

First published 1997
02 01 00 99 98 97     5 4 3 2 1

Permissions appear on page 193

Library of Congress Cataloging-in-Publication Data
Chidvilasananda, Gurumayi.
Enthusiasm / Swami Chidvilasananda.
p. cm.
"A Siddha Yoga publication."
Includes bibliographical references and index.
ISBN 0-911307-52-4 (pbk. : alk. paper)
1. Spiritual life. 2. Enthusiasm—Religious aspects. I. Title.
BP610.C4814 1997
294.5'44—dc21 97-3130
CIP

Printed on recycled paper that meets the American National Standard for Permanence of Paper for Printed Library Materials.

# CONTENTS

## *The Siddha Yoga Tradition*

Swami Chidvilasananda is a Siddha Master, an enlightened teacher who initiates and guides seekers on the spiritual path. Heir to an ancient lineage of Siddhas, Swami Chidvilasananda received the power to transmit spiritual energy from her Master, Swami Muktananda. At the instruction of his Guru, the revered saint Bhagawan Nityananda, Swami Muktananda brought the previously secret experience of *shaktipāt* initiation to the West during the last twelve years of his life.

Since her Guru's passing in 1982, Swami Chidvilasananda, known as Gurumayi, has continued in this tradition, traveling widely, freely bestowing the spiritual awakening of *shaktipāt,* and guiding the development of seekers throughout the world. Wherever Gurumayi goes, whatever she says, whatever actions she performs, she conveys the Siddhas' message that the experience of divine Consciousness is attainable in this human body. Fulfillment is already yours, Gurumayi assures us; you need only look for it in the right place — deep within your own heart.

On the path of Siddha Yoga this experience of completion, the freedom of perfect contentment, comes through the exquisite interplay between the Master's grace and the seeker's effort. Eventually the seeker becomes aware of his or her own perfection and perceives the bond of love that unites each one of us with God. This is the promise and blessing of the lineage of Siddha Yoga Masters.

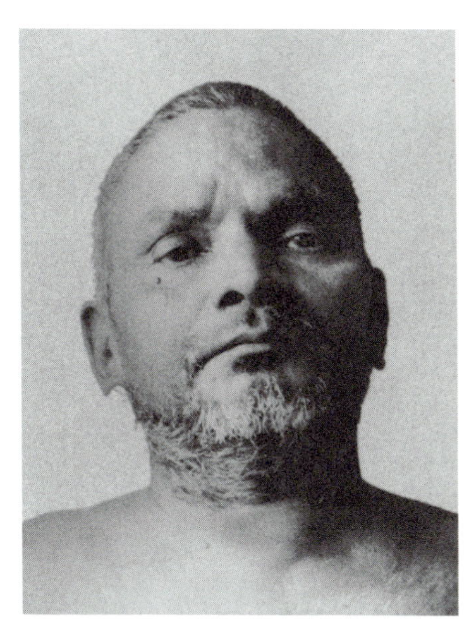

BHAGAWAN NITYANANDA

SWAMI MUKTANANDA

# *Introduction*

During the year 1996, Gurumayi Chidvilasananda gave a series of talks now gathered in this volume. Her talks began with a New Year's message, "Be filled with enthusiasm and sing God's glory": that message reverberates in various ways through all the subsequent chapters of the book. While each of the talks included here was given during the course of one year, their primary resonance for this reader is not with the events of that particular year, but with a much greater sweep of time and with kindred spirits whose geographic range is global. Let me share a few of my impressions of the broad — indeed universal — themes that we encounter in the chapters of *Enthusiasm.*

Most immediately, I am struck by the vividness of Gurumayi's images, by the way she does what all great teachers do, which is to place a seed — often visual — that stays with the student/reader long after the lesson is over. In the case at hand, the seeds are sometimes not even central to the line of thought (or line of heart!) she is developing. But they are woven into the text. And they linger. So I find myself haunted by the idea that the amount of light that the morning sun can flood into a house is a function of whether the curtains are open or closed. And also by the image of the Self as an anchor that keeps a boat pointed into the wind, secure against the buffetings of wind and tide. The image of a buffalo wallowing contentedly in the mud it has dredged up from a beautiful, lotus-filled pond, as a model for someone who lives mired in self-hatred, perhaps depends on having marveled at such buffaloes in India, but the notion of someone building a castle of garbage and then choosing to live in it makes the lesson universal.

A further response I have to these talks is based on having read a great deal of mystical literature over the years and having regularly taught a course, now for over twenty years, entitled "Mystical Experience, Eastern and Western." In discussions, we naturally pay attention to important theoretical issues, but at the heart of this course has always been extensive reading of primary texts written by or about mystics: the words of these spiritual virtuosi themselves. These remarkable individuals have lived in every time and place (though more in some than others), and they have shared an understanding that human life is fundamentally a spiritual phenomenon. In order for any of us to live fully, they intuit — actually they know — we must go deeper than the conventional understanding of humans as bundles of desires, conditioned by social or political or economic or psychological or other forces. There is an inner divinity, they attest, whose reality can be known at first hand, knowledge of which renders all other knowledge secondary. And the most astonishing thing about that divinity, the mystics say, is that it is one's own inner Self, one's own most private person, properly understood. What they offer is testimony to the reality of this innermost deity/Self and techniques for coming to know it. In encountering the talks in this volume, which grow out of Gurumayi's own experience, I am struck by the fact that they place her squarely in the company of these mystics. She frequently cites like-hearted individuals who are Muslim, Jewish, Chinese, Christian, and Buddhist, as well as Hindu. They are all "kindred spirits" in the literal sense of those words: individuals who are related to one another through the spirit. Theirs is a community, not in the physical sense, but in the sense of a shared aspiration, a shared intent, and frequently (but not always) a shared experience. They are, at a minimum, pointing in the same direction.

It is at this point that I ask myself whether we ought not to apply the word *genius* to these mystics. After all, we readily apply such a characterization to certain individuals whose lives and talents have enriched others in a great variety of ways, most especially in the arts. Mozart in music, Milton or Tulsidas or Matsuo Basho in poetry, Michelangelo or the anonymous sculptors of Gupta Age Buddha figures — they all provide intimations of a "more," of a grace and beauty and wonder and mystery that raises the rest of us to another level, showing us things that we have only dimly glimpsed. How much more is that the case with regard to these spiritual virtuosi! Would our lives not be immeasurably impoverished if they had not lived? As I try to envision a human history without these kindred spirits, past and present, what a bleak and cold place it would be! I am happy to call them friends, to acknowledge how enriched my own life has been by their genius.

The results of genius, whether artistic or spiritual, are, of course, wondrously diverse. Similarly the paths that cultivate genius in all of its forms vary significantly. It is in this light, I think, that we should understand Gurumayi's emphasis on the range of ways that sadhana, spiritual practice, manifests itself. In particular, while noting the dramatic visions and *kriyās* often associated with mystical experience, Gurumayi also raises up for comment the modest, rather unspectacular deepening of daily experience. This latter kind of mystical experience finds its roots not so much in spectacular alterations of consciousness, but in a deepening certitude, a quiet confidence and knowledge that the whole of the universe and of human life is constructed on the reality of God. I have found it useful in my own teaching to distinguish between "high incandescence" and "low incandescence" mystics. The former know a spiritual path that is filled with ecstasy, passion, intense longing, and occasionally anguish (one thinks perhaps of Rumi or Blake) while the latter, no less spiritual, just differently spiritual (one thinks of certain Upanishadic sayings or Teilhard de Chardin) find themselves rooted ever more solidly in the quiet knowledge of God's reality, God's ubiquity. Gurumayi, too, is reminding us that, while mystics may indeed all be pointed in the same direction, there is an enormously rich variety in their individual experiences. She urges each spiritual aspirant to develop his or her own sadhana, not to compare it with others. We ought not to assume that the highly incandescent form of mystical experience, for all its intensity, is the only form. Gradual growth in gentle certainty of God is also part of the genus — and the genius — of mystical experience.

Finally, I am struck by the fact that in these talks, at a very down-to-earth level that requires no knowledge of the universal community of mystics and does not demand immediate susceptibility to spirituality, we have a powerful series of reflections on how one goes about living a life of integrity. Put aspirations to transcendence aside. Forego overt language about God. Forget — at least for the time being — ceremony, sadhana, meditation, and overt forms of religiousness. Then ask: how does one cope with the slings and arrows of the world? How does one relate to one's fellows? How does one try to make the world a better place, for oneself and for others? How does one remain true to oneself? Gurumayi has a host of trenchant thoughts on these matters, worthy of being taken to heart by all who seek to move beyond the banality of ordinary life. The great Muslim intellectual and mystic al-Ghazali once claimed that he learned more about practicing the presence of God from an unlettered peasant woman working in the fields outside Baghdad than he did from all the learned intellectuals in the academy. Just so, Gurumayi reminds us that spirituality is not the exclusive property of specialists. What has been known most vividly by spiritual geniuses is, in fact, accessible to all thoughtful, heartful people.

Surely it is no accident, then, that the focus for this year's message is *enthusiasm.* On the surface it is a remarkably innocent word. But it is a word of great power, precisely because we can imagine becoming enthusiastic about a great range of activities, many of which are not overtly religious or spiritual. *Enthusiasm* is a word with the potential to cut across the conventional dualities of life — as mystics are forever aspiring to do in their movement toward unity! But first the word needs to be rescued from the "spin doctors" and cheerleaders of the world, for whom enthusiasm is something to be manufactured, constructed for a particular end, for whom the end justifies the means. Gurumayi does this, just as she rescues other words from their conventional trivialization — *freedom of speech, patience, forgiveness,* and others. Bit by bit, piece by piece, she then reconstructs a deeper, truer meaning for these familiar notions. She shows how a life of authentic enthusiasm, of genuine "enspiritedness," is its own reward.

*Thomas B. Coburn*
*St. Lawrence University*

***Thomas B. Coburn** is a historian of religion, specializing in the study of South Asia. The author of two books on the Hindu Goddess, he is the Charles A. Dana Professor of Religious Studies at St. Lawrence University, where he has taught since 1974 and where he currently serves as Vice President of the University and Dean of Academic Affairs.*

## *A Note on the Text*

In the text, Sanskrit and Hindi terms appear in italics unless they are words frequently used in Siddha Yoga publications. In the Glossary of Texts and Terms, all Sanskrit words appear with transliteration according to the international standard. Sanskrit scriptural passages and the first lines of Hindi and Marathi songs appear in the Notes with the same standard transliteration. Accompanying the Notes is a Guide to Sanskrit Pronunciation.

*Chapter 1*

# Be Filled with Enthusiasm and Sing God's Glory

With great respect, with great love, I welcome you all with all my heart.

Another wondrous year has begun. What does it hold for you? What great magic will it reveal? What destiny will it unfold before your eyes? What treasures does it contain? Will it live up to your highest hopes and fulfill your deepest yearnings? What does the coming year carry in its womb for you?

There is another way to look at this. How are *you* planning to welcome the new year? Have you prepared yourself to receive the coming year in the most auspicious way? Instead of pinning all your expectations on the new year, have you thought of doing something about the way you greet the future? Are you prepared to let bygones be bygones? Are you completely ready to take a new step forward?

The followers of Siddha Yoga teachings like to know at the beginning of each new year if there is a particular message for the whole year that they can imbibe and put into practice. Siddha Yoga is the yoga of grace, the abundant grace of the Master. Freely and spontaneously this grace enters the lives of seekers. Yet for the Guru's grace to unfold in its fullness, it demands that seekers put forth a sincere effort to reach the goal of their seeking. Therefore, the message for this year calls for both benevolent grace and sweet effort. The New Year's message is "Be filled with enthusiasm and sing God's glory."

Enthusiasm dances in the bloodstream of the great saints

and sages and all the true leaders of the world. Enthusiasm enables a person to realize his goal. Enthusiasm makes you soar. When you become aware of your own great capacity for enthusiasm, you realize there is something sacred within you. Why is this?

The answer is contained in the word itself. If you trace it back to its roots, you discover that the word *enthusiasm* comes from the Greek *enthusiasmos.* The syllable *en* means "in, within, or possessed." And *theos* means "God." So the word *enthusiasm* literally means "carrying God within" or "possessed of the inner Lord." When you are filled with enthusiasm, you are filled with the energy of God, with great power, with amazing grace. To become fully conscious of what you are carrying inside is to inherit all of heaven. This awareness frees you completely from worry. You are filled with God. What can possibly dampen your spirit? This new understanding of the word *enthusiasm* evokes a deep longing within you.

The question is, how can you make this divine quality stream forth within you? By singing God's glory. When you sing God's glory, you become filled with enthusiasm. And when you are filled with enthusiasm, then you sing God's glory as spontaneously as water flows in a stream after a bountiful rainfall. Each part of the New Year's message is complete in itself, and each one also leads to the other.

In his book *Play of Consciousness*, Baba Muktananda says, "Enthusiasm and energy are very helpful friends in this world." You must have noticed how you are spontaneously drawn toward people who are enthusiastic. When someone is full of exuberance and vigor, you want to be around them. Which one creates greater *rasa*, a greater flavor of life, the sight of a dry withered leaf or a fresh green leaf? If you see a depressed person and a happy person, which one of them generates a feeling of newness inside you? If you come across a gloomy face and a happy face, with whom do you want to talk? If you have a choice between two conversations — one that is depressing, sullen, and argumentative, or one that is filled with energy, laughter, goodwill, and eagerness — toward which conversation will you gravitate? There is an inherent impulse in every human being to move forward to a place, to a person, or to a time that is sparkling with enthusiasm, with God's energy.

To be filled with enthusiasm means to give yourself completely to God and let God steer the wheel of your life. Everyone wants his or her life to be full of purpose. In fact, many people ask: "What is the purpose of my life? How can I know the purpose of my life?" Everyone is looking for a way to live that is meaningful, dedicated, and full of wonder, *chamatkāra.* Everyone wants to be full of happiness and love, to lead a harmonious life with great friends, sweet pleasures, a feeling of abundance, and great wisdom, uninterrupted by loss. Everyone really does want all this.

However, most people seem to look for meaning outside themselves. They think that abundance, purpose, and pleasure are hiding somewhere else in the world and they need to go and hunt for them. They forget that each human being is the pivotal factor in his or her own life. Each person holds within himself that which he is seeking. In order to make your life the way you want it to be, you have to become filled with enthusiasm. You have to become the perfect vessel to carry the golden light of grace.

So you don't have to leave it to fate to decide what the coming year will hold for you. If you make the best of each moment, then every year becomes the greatest and most wonder-filled year of your life.

Once, in response to a seeker's question, Baba Muktananda said: "Whatever you acquire in the outer world will ultimately leave you weak and feeble. There is only one thing that will make you stronger day by day, that will release more and more enthusiasm within you, and that is the Guru's grace. As you pass into meditation through your Guru's grace, you find your life becoming sweeter and happier." To visualize enthusiasm being released within you through the grace of the Guru is a great *dhāranā*, a centering technique.

Baba was always filled with enthusiasm. That was one of the things that drew people to him. Enthusiasm poured out of Baba — when he was in the kitchen cooking, when he was playing with a child or talking to people, when he was looking at the ocean or giving a scholarly commentary on a scripture, when he was studying alone at his desk, or when something was humorous. Just as the ocean roars, enthusiasm roared within Baba. Whether he was watering a plant or giving instructions to a sevite, whether he was gazing out at space or sitting quietly in the courtyard, you could experience unbounded enthusiasm streaming from him, washing you clean, filling you with a sense of the glory of life. You felt life moving inside you when you watched him, whether he was in action or just sitting quietly.

When Baba strolled through the gardens or sang the name of God, when he gave profound advice or greeted a visitor, you could feel his unimpeded enthusiasm, the exuberance that was dancing within him. Whenever you caught even a glimpse of his brilliant orange robes on the other side of the upper garden of Gurudev Siddha Peeth, our mother ashram in India, you felt a tremendous flood of enthusiasm pouring out of him. From the first thing in the morning till the last thing at night, Baba's entire day was lived with enthusiasm. He was always bright eyed. His entire being pulsated with great wonder. When you saw him, you wanted to know more about life. Enthusiasm is what Baba taught. He would say, "Do your work with enthusiasm. Chant God's name with enthusiasm. Let there be enthusiasm in your being." Baba's enthusiasm was contagious. To be with Baba was to be full of Baba's joy.

A scholar of Kashmir Shaivism, commenting on the teachings of the sage Utpaladeva, writes: "Wonder is the essence of life. To be incapable of wonder is to be as dead and insensitive as a stone. We live and enjoy the vitality (*vīrya*) of consciousness to the degree in which we are sensitive to the beauty of things around us."[1] Each aesthetic experience should be enjoyed mindfully and with a disciplined intention. This intention is directed toward heightening the general level of our sensitivity to beauty. In that way, every bit of beauty that you encounter will bring you a little closer to a sustained sense of wonder. This wonder is the pulsation of Consciousness that permeates all experience. The scholar continues his commentary: "A yogi at first practices to penetrate into this state of wonder through the medium of objects more easily pleasing and then, as he makes progress, he learns to discern that same sense of wonder in himself, even when confronted with the foulest of things or in times of great trouble and pain."

This is what Baba Muktananda continually taught us. Whenever we got upset as young children, Baba would call us and say, "Look! Isn't this stone beautiful!" And we would look at the object and think, "A mere stone." He would say, "Look, this is so beautiful!" We looked at him and looked at the stone. And then he would laugh, and within a few seconds we would be laughing too. As soon as we started laughing, we could see that the stone was in fact so beautiful. Baba showed us the great wonder in simple things. And he completely changed our mood, our way of thinking, by infusing great wonder into these simple things.

After we received *shaktipāt*, we found out that people can have dramatic experiences if they continue meditating. But we noticed that our meditations weren't that deep or dramatic. We were just sitting quietly. So we became a little restless and we walked around the ashram with long faces. We felt our meditations weren't really going that well. Baba would unfailingly find out what we were feeling. You see, the ashram was very small in those days, and Baba had an invisible magnifying glass — at least that's what *we* thought. And so, he invited us to come to the courtyard where he was sitting, and he asked, "How's your meditation going?"

Of course, we weren't eager to describe our meditation experiences. So we just sat there and looked at him. He said, "Your meditation is great?"

Finally, we said with downcast eyes, "No."

"No? Your meditation is not good? What do you mean? When do you meditate?"

Baba asked lots of questions, and we tried to answer them as well as we could. Then he said, "That's wonderful! You are so fortunate! You are so lucky!"

We thought, "Really? Just to be able to sit quietly is wonderful?" We had never realized that. Just to sit quietly *is* meditation. That really is a great attainment, just to sit quietly for a couple of hours. We became infused with this novel idea that to sit quietly for two hours without going anywhere was a dramatic experience.

Baba continued to say how wonderful it was and how fortunate we were, and we completely melted into his enthusiasm — about our boring meditation sessions. And then we went back to our daily meditations with so much enthusiasm. In fact, we woke up singing because we were so happy to go and sit for meditation — just to sit quietly for a couple of hours.

So you start with simple things, and then you carry your enthusiasm to greater and greater realms. You carry the wonder-filled attitude into every moment, into every action, and you experience your own boundless enthusiasm.

As a true seeker you must develop this sense of wonder. Everything in God's universe is a cause for wonder. You must be able to experience awe and respect for all the forms of life around you. Then you will be able to maintain your enthusiasm. This means never feeling dull or at a loss, never feeling lethargic or defeated, never feeling helpless or betrayed, never feeling dead or deserted. When you go to work, go with a sense of wonder: "Oh, how is the office going to be today? Who will I meet today? What conversations will take place? What wonderful work is waiting for me?"

When you contemplate in this way, enthusiasm comes and presents itself before you. When you go to meet someone, have this sense of wonder: "Who will I meet? How will the meeting be? What will be the outcome?" Don't walk into the office thinking, "Do I really want to see that woman's face again? Oh, so much paperwork. What will I do?" No! Go to your office eager to find out: "How many more projects can I look into? How much more paperwork can be put in order? What is the best way to accomplish the work?" And when you go shopping don't disparage everything on the shelves. Let the market be filled with wonder. "Those artichokes — aren't they wonderful! That cashier — isn't she nice! The person over there, she's my neighbor. I'll go help her. She is always so kind to me." And when you are driving somewhere, instead of dreading all the traffic, find ways to create a wonderful satsang for yourself. "I hope I don't have to drive too fast, because I want to listen to this new chanting tape. I hope I have a lot of time in the car to chant all the way."

A little child constantly experiences wonder. Everything about life tingles and activates curiosity in the being of a child. Children come into this world with an inner smile and eyes that want to grasp the magic of the universe. Being with children, parents relive their youth, whatever their age may be. This sense of wonder, which is the essence of life, continually creates fresh life. As a modern writer once said, "So long as enthusiasm lasts, so long is youth still with us." Be filled with enthusiasm and sing God's glory.

You can fill your entire year with enthusiasm. Begin now by welcoming the year with your whole heart. Who knows? It may be filled with wondrous teachings, magical insights, marvelous experiences and encounters. Whatever it brings, adopt a yogic attitude and discern the same sense of wonder within your own self. Whatever the year presents you with, remember to sing God's glory. Keep the name of God on the tip of your tongue. Relish its ineffable beauty. Let this year be the most wonder-filled year.

Welcome this sense of wonder into every aspect of your life. When you first wake up in the morning, greet the day with praise: "What a glorious, grace-filled morning! What a wondrous feeling I have inside! *Om Namah Shivāya!* Awake I am! May the entire day be filled with God's wisdom!" Visualize the happy face of your Guru. Hear the strains of the mantra echoing inside you. With great wonder, look forward to what the next moment will bring. Visualize every cell in your body filled with vitality. As Baba Muktananda would say, "Vitality is coursing through every blood corpuscle." Let this vitality assist you, let it see you through the day.

As you breathe in and breathe out, become filled with more and more enthusiasm. God's glory is flowing in your veins. God's glory is singing through all your actions. Let this energy guide you throughout your day. Do not judge whether what you are doing is impressive or mediocre, spiritual or mundane. Just do it with enthusiasm. Just give yourself to whatever you do with this full knowledge: "God is within me. All actions that I perform are offerings to Him. Whatever He wants to do with me, let Him do it as He wills." Have the certainty that God is with you, that you carry God's energy, and that all your actions are in praise of Him. Walk happily. Speak sweetly. Do everything diligently. Be meticulous in every dealing. Let dharma support you.

Baba Muktananda used to say: "Always remember your own inner Self with great love. Always think of the dazzling flame of love that is present inside you. That flame will fill you with great delight, great happiness, great zest."

How do you experience this dazzling flame of love? Through singing God's glory. This doesn't mean just sitting in one place and chanting the name of God. Singing God's glory is allowing your entire being to send forth God's beauty, God's bounty, God's love. You must let God's energy flow into every minute of your day. That is singing God's glory.

In the *Rāmāyana*, Hanuman, the great devotee of the Lord, says:

> Any moment spent without singing God's name and glory should be regarded as a great loss. That moment is a moment of ignorance and delusion.[2]

Singing God's name is singing His glory. Chanting the mantra is singing God's glory. But isn't there another even more meaningful way to sing God's glory? Isn't there another means that is very pleasing to God? Yes, there is. There is a splendid path by following which you truly do sing God's glory. To experience God's perfection in all the people you meet is to sing His glory. When you meet people, instead of sizing them up and down, look for the great virtues they carry within them. Begin to appreciate every little thing they do. That will make it easier for you to recognize the great things they are capable of. Allow yourself to acknowledge the goodness you see in each person. That is singing God's glory.

When you see a beautiful plant, let yourself feel its loveliness and thank God for its existence.

When you see the sun rise and set, let yourself be engulfed by its majesty spreading across the sky. Watch it display the most unearthly combination of colors — each sunrise, unique; each sunset, unrepeatable. Thank God for the existence of the sun. Understand that each one of your days is just as incomparable and just as heavenly.

When you see the stars and the moon in the night sky, let yourself be overcome by tender feelings, and thank God for their existence.

When you receive compliments from others, let them warm your heart, and thank God for His grace in that form.

When you are afflicted with troubles and unexpected calamities, thank God for their existence too. Know full well that He will protect you and that He wants you to extract a lesson or two from them. That is singing God's glory.

When you expect people to do something for you and they don't come through, feel good about them anyway. Don't change your good opinion about them. That is singing God's glory.

When nothing seems to go the way you want, continue to maintain your inner composure, your inner delight, and offer your gratitude to God. Perhaps God wants it some other way. That is singing God's glory.

God's power is *shrī*. It is filled with auspiciousness, beauty, sacredness, abundance, nobility, dignity, and good fortune. When you allow your actions to be suffused with these qualities of *shrī*, you are singing God's glory.

When you allow your good understanding and virtues to guide your words and actions, rather than letting your attention be led away by lack of understanding, then you are singing God's glory.

When you take the time to speak with someone who is seeking spiritual upliftment and tell her about your inner experience of God's love and grace, you are singing God's glory.

When you recognize unconditional love flashing forth in someone's smile; in a gesture of kindness; in his steady, helping hand; in her cheerful spirits; don't let the chance slip by. Take a moment to express your love. This is singing God's glory.

When someone awakens great love in your heart, don't just keep it for yourself, thinking, "Oh, her love is meant just for me." Acknowledge such a loving nature. That is singing God's glory.

When you meet someone who has worked very hard for the benefit of many people, who has given his or her best to the world, don't presume that your appreciation is immediately felt. Take a moment to express your gratitude, your heartfelt appreciation. This is magnifying God's beauty, God's abundance, God's sacredness. It is spreading good fortune everywhere and singing God's glory.

Whenever your actions express the inner magnificence of the heart, the inner auspiciousness, the inner spiritual power, you are singing God's glory.

Right now, in this very moment, you can allow yourself to experience an ocean of enthusiasm and the continuous pulsation of God's glory in your own being. You can experience your Self. Just feel your own body; your own being carries the energy of God, enthusiasm. You don't have to wait for the circumstances to be impeccable and perfect. You simply make a decision: "I am going to let God's energy pour through me. I am going to make all the space in my heart, all the space in my being, available for God. I am going to walk through the day and night seeing God's presence everywhere around me and allowing His energy to work through me." Let the sense of wonder be constant. It's just a simple resolution.

Remembering God is singing God's glory. Repeating His name is singing His glory. Seeing God in each other is singing God's glory. Respecting God in each other is singing God's glory. Understanding and worshiping God in each other is singing God's glory. Loving God in each other and being generous with each other is singing God's glory. Showing kindness to each other is singing God's glory. Expressing gratitude to each other is singing God's glory. Then, in turn, you experience His rewards as great enthusiasm, zest, and ecstasy.

When enthusiasm courses through your veins, when music dances in every cell of your body, you become a beacon of light for this world. Everyone around you is happy — automatically. You don't have to roam from continent to continent trying to fulfill yourself. Fulfillment is already yours. You carry the vessel of fulfillment. Then wherever you go, you have something to offer others. This is singing God's glory.

In his book *From the Finite to the Infinite*, Baba Muktananda says: "This is why we live: to experience supreme bliss, the highest enthusiasm, the highest ecstasy. A human life is mysterious and significant; it is sublime and ideal. In this human body, in this human life, we can see the Creator within, we can meet Him and talk to Him, and we can also become Him."

Sit quietly for a few moments and visualize God's energy coursing through your entire body. The body has its own subtle vibration that you can experience. You may feel it on your skin or deep in the marrow of your bones. When you allow your entire being to become still in its own subtle vibration, you can experience God's power. It is *shrī*. It is filled with auspiciousness, beauty, sacredness, abundance, nobility, dignity, and good fortune. Know that all this exists within yourself.

Give yourself this gift throughout the year: experience your own *shrī*, your own auspiciousness, your own beauty, your own sacredness, your own abundance, your own nobility and dignity, your own good fortune. Let every virtue in you blossom. Let every hidden good quality of yours shine forth. Immerse yourself in your own *shrī*, and emerge with the blossoms of *shrī*. Be filled with enthusiasm and sing God's glory.

With great respect, with great love, I welcome you all with all my heart.

*Sadgurunāth mahārāj kī jay!*

*Chapter 2*

# We Are Born of God's Ecstasy

With great respect, with great love, I welcome you all with all my heart.

The Upanishads say that one day God had a thought, "Let Me become many." And He became many. The One became many. What must it have been like? What must God have felt when His wish for this universe came into existence? First there was the initial *spanda*, the divine throb, the great pulsation, the stirring of life in the void. This became simmering heat within a tiny seed that we call the Blue Pearl. Then finally, God let it go forth.

This is an amazing *dhāranā* to practice: we are actually born out of God's ecstasy. We are completely wrapped in His ecstasy, sustained in His ecstasy. We are the source of His enthusiasm, and we are the product of His enthusiasm. We are His enthusiasm, and we are His universe. We *are* God's enthusiasm. Can you believe it? God is truly happy with us.

Have you ever imagined how far the outpouring of God's enthusiasm might extend? Stretch your imagination. Recently someone told me about a report from astronomers who are studying photographs taken through a space telescope. They have discovered that there are five times as many galaxies in the universe as had been previously estimated. This means there are about fifty billion galaxies. If there were only one Earthlike planet per galaxy — which is said to be an extremely conservative estimate — there would be fifty billion Earthlike planets in the universe. And that means there would be nine such planets for every single person who is alive on this Earth today.

Have you ever thought of matching your enthusiasm with God's enthusiasm? Take a deep breath. Have you ever imagined yourself dancing in the luminous sphere of His boundless enthusiasm? You may say it is inconceivable; the physical body simply could not survive the impact of God's power. Yet the most amazing thing is, when you truly let yourself become filled with divine luminosity, it is no different from God's enthusiasm. When you experience incredible resilience in every circumstance of your life, you are living in God's enthusiasm. You are filled with enthusiasm when you are silent. You are filled with enthusiasm when you perform actions. You are filled with enthusiasm when you show kindness and when you experience complete detachment. In all these ways, very naturally, you are singing God's glory.

To melt into His enthusiasm and be the song in His heart, to melt into His eyes and be the vision of His sight, to surrender into His hands and be His servant, to merge into His love and be His beloved is to embrace His enthusiasm and sing His glory through all of time and eternity. So melt into His eyes and be the vision of His sight. Embrace God's enthusiasm.

An ancient hymn to Lord Shiva, written by Utpaladeva, a sage of Kashmir Shaivism, expresses and invokes the inconceivable glory of the Lord:

> May you be glorified
> Who have made manifest your grandeur
> By placing your signet
> On each and every thing in this world.
> May you be glorified, Great Lord,
> Lord of the universe into which
> You have infused your own soul. . . .

May you be glorified,
The only lamp for worldly beings
Blinded by the darkness of delusion.
May you be glorified, O Supreme Person,
Ever awake in the midst of a sleeping world. . . .

Being self-luminous
You cause everything to shine;
Delighting in your form
You fill the universe with delight;
Rocking with your own bliss
You make the whole world dance with joy.[1]

Did you know you have all been imbued with the luster of enthusiasm? Truly, it shines through every cell of your body all day and through the darkest of nights. You are a bundle of enthusiasm, you carry God within. The word *enthusiasm* literally means "possessed of the inner Lord," possessed of His light. This expresses itself as eagerness, exuberance, vitality, buoyancy, optimism, and ecstasy. It is the radiant glow of the inner fire. It is your intense determination to recognize God's love in your own life that has brought you to the spiritual path.

Each of you, in your own unique way, must have experienced different degrees of enthusiasm. Sometimes you may not even realize how enthusiastic you are, but others can feel it. You may think you are dragging your feet, but others can feel great energy emanating from your being. Sometimes you experience enthusiasm consciously because you know you are filled with joy. At other times you don't recognize it because you think you are lonely and empty. At times your enthusiasm is expressed deliberately and at other times haphazardly. As you explore the innumerable ways of singing God's glory, you discover what it truly means. Enthusiasm doesn't mean just screaming and shouting at the top of your lungs. When you are filled with enthusiasm sometimes you are deeply silent in your own being — when you pray, when you work, when you spend time in nature.

Baba Muktananda reminds us again and again, "The purpose of our lives is to experience supreme bliss, the highest enthusiasm, the highest ecstasy." However, until you experience complete union with God, the restlessness within your own being is unbearable. The restlessness you experience is not just because your mind is wandering, not just because you aren't getting what you want in this world. This restlessness is very deeply rooted: it comes from the experience of separation from God, separation from God's love. When you truly look deep into your heart, it is the separation between you and your Beloved, you and your God, that causes this incredible discomfort, this restlessness.

If you have not experienced union with God, the myriad things you try to do will only amount to thousands of zeroes without a number preceding them to give them value. That union, that completion, comes about once you have begun to give yourself completely to God deep in your heart. This is not an external posture. It happens on the inside. Sometimes people think if you love God, then everything on the outside should reflect the beauty, the glory, the magnificence, and so on. They think if it doesn't, you're not experiencing God. However, the experience of God is a mysterious and internal event. Sometimes your face may even look gloomy; it may not reveal at all what is happening on the inside.

There are some sadhus in India who practice looking very melancholy. They show complete distaste for the world, absolute detachment from every object. Yet on the inside they do attain God's love, they do merge into God. It is mysterious. So don't look for signs only on the outside. On the other hand, the experience does overflow; the inner enthusiasm will overflow into your outer life. Let it happen naturally. You don't have to try to pluck it from inside and plant it on the outside so the whole world can see how enthusiastic you are. Let it grow on the inside. Just let it happen. God is pleased when your thoughts, words, and actions originate from His energy flowing deep inside you.

In the central episode of the great Indian epic called the *Rāmāyana*, Lord Rama's pure-hearted queen, Sita, is kidnapped by a demon. Lord Rama is distraught. He searches the length of the land for his queen but to no avail. With the passage of time, he becomes inconsolable and loses the inspiration to search further. His companion can see that if Rama drowns in his sorrow, Sita will never be rescued. He tells Lord Rama:

> Maintain the auspicious state of mind that is your own true nature. A lost object is not retrieved except by effort. Hence, we should cultivate enthusiasm. Enthusiasm is the greatest power. For a man endowed with enthusiasm, nothing in this world is impossible to achieve. A man with enthusiasm does not despair in action. We shall regain Sita by recourse to enthusiastic action, O Rama. Give up this sorrow born of affection, which has unfortunately veiled your own supreme glory.[2]

This is a pivotal point and a very profound teaching about how to experience your own enthusiasm and how to sing God's glory with your heart completely open. Although maintaining the auspicious state of mind may sound like a very difficult task, it is still the greatest endeavor one can make on the spiritual path. Just because it is an arduous process and requires constant vigilance doesn't mean you should feel it is more than you can handle. Feeling overwhelmed is such a tendency of the mind, isn't it? If something is difficult, the mind thinks, "Oh my goodness, I'm so overwhelmed by this. I can't do it." If you can succeed in maintaining the auspicious state of mind, then you will find yourself holding God's glory in your own golden hands. Wherever your hands turn, you will be pouring the delicious nectar of God's light. Wherever your mind goes, you will be spreading the mantle of God's love.

The knowers of the Truth repeatedly say: "Sing God's glory. Extend kindness. Look at others with love. See God in each other. Understand what others are experiencing." You will become free from the snares of the world and regain your freedom by singing God's glory, by planting the seeds of God's love everywhere, by helping others and knowing it is God's hand that is doing everything. Your heart will be so light and you will become everything you ever wanted to be. Then you will know the most natural way to chant the glorious name of the Lord. You will continually hum the song of the Lord. Singing God's glory means being there for people. Singing God's glory means recognizing God's ways.

How else do the saints and sages sing God's glory? Here is their secret: they are able to perceive and honor the attributes of God in all the people they meet.

Once someone asked Baba Muktananda, "What is it you see when a person comes before you?"

Baba said, "First and foremost, I see the Blue Pearl shining brilliantly in each person." What a divine vision. The saints are able to see the goodness in each person, and that is what they want people to recognize within themselves. Their experience becomes their mission: to awaken that power within each person so that everyone can come to understand his own divine glory within.

There is a story from the *Mahābhārata* that offers a hint about how to see the world as the saints do. In ancient India there were two leaders who had mastered their respective skills. One was the prince Duryodhana, who had become proficient in the art of seeing faults in others. He had used his God-given intelligence to plot against his cousins and to fatten his greed and ambition. To this end, he had courted the six enemies: desire, anger, greed, pride, delusion, and jealousy.

The other was the great leader Yudhishthira, who had spent his life cultivating the divine virtues and letting them guide his actions. He was completely devoted to dharma, the path of righteousness.

One day there was a vast assembly of people. Lord Krishna was present along with Duryodhana and Yudhishthira. When everyone was seated, the Lord turned to Duryodhana and said, "You are such a great king, Duryodhana; you have such great intelligence. Please select a truly virtuous soul from this huge assembly and show him to me."

Hardly casting a glance around the hall, Duryodhana answered quickly: "Krishna, don't be so naive. I know these people well. Every one of them is ruthless and selfish. I know how they think. Let me tell you, there is not a single virtuous soul in this assembly."

Lord Krishna smiled and turned to Yudhishthira, saying: "Please point out someone in this assembly who is wicked through and through."

Without a moment's hesitation, Yudhishthira replied: "Lord, this is a gathering of fine people, great scholars, wise men and women. It is an honor to know them. Their hearts are full of noble virtues. Before them I am not even a blade of grass. They are people of good will and lofty aspirations. There is no one here, O my Lord, whom I would call wicked."

Two perceptions. What you see depends on how you cultivate your heart, how you keep your mind. When you perceive the world with divine vision, you can think of anyone, and that person will be suffused with God's love. You can touch anything, and that object will be imbued with God's energy.

Take a moment now and visualize someone who is very dear to you. The person may be alive or dead, close or far away. Having visualized this person, begin to recall his or her good qualities. Each time this person demonstrated some good quality, what did you feel? How has this good quality affected your life? Each time you spoke about this quality to someone else, what did you feel? What kind of environment did it create? Each time you met this person, remembering this good quality, how did your meeting go? Each time you let the person know how much you benefited from the good quality, to what level of consciousness did you ascend? Every time you brought this person's good quality to the forefront of your mind, how did you react? Being totally free from jealousy, linger on this good quality of the one who is dear to you.

Doesn't this practice fill you with enthusiasm, with the satisfaction of singing God's glory? To honor God in another person is to sing His glory. It is letting God know you respect and love Him because you see Him throughout His creation. To honor another person is to sing God's glory unconditionally. Now allow that same wondrous quality to permeate your own being.

When you become aware of how to sing God's glory through every thought, every word, and every action, you become aware of God's power within you. You come to understand that saintliness is not a gift that God confers on merely a chosen few. Rather, it is a treasure that God has placed within every child of His. The Indian poet-saint Brahmananda says:

> O lover, don't go searching outside.
> The Beloved dwells inside your body.
>
> When the gaze of the sun, moon, and stars falls upon
> the supremely enchanting radiance of the Beloved,
> they feel bashful. They know the great radiance.
>
> Brahmananda beholds this unearthly brilliance
> whose auspiciousness and bliss
> pervades everything.[3]

Now think of someone who has been unpleasant to you, who has done many wrongs to you, someone whom you think of as your enemy. Visualize this person. He or she may be a lifelong enemy or a recent enemy. Recall one good quality that this person has. Just one. Let this good quality of your enemy permeate your being. Experience the power of this one single good quality of your enemy. Relish its sweetness. Perceive its crystalline beauty. Discover its strength. If such a great quality exists in this person, how can he or she be so bad?

Consider this: if there is one shining quality in that person, there must be many other wonderful qualities hidden inside as well. These qualities are worth more than all the precious gems in the world. Just as one single diamond can radiate effulgence, this single good quality of your enemy can radiate God's essence. Therefore, instead of looking at this person with anger or indifference, try looking in a different way, a new way — although from the viewpoint of your great Self, it is not really new. Just imagine that your eyes have been washed with holy water, that God has sweetly touched your eyes. Now perceive this good quality, which you have magnified with your own generous heart. Adorn this person with the brilliant attire of this quality as seen through your own eyes. Feed him or her with the delicious food of this quality. Be nurturing. Speak to the person with the sweet music of this good quality. Let this person know what you see; offer back the good quality that you have uncovered.

Look at what you truly feel toward this person. What is the state of your heart? What is your inner connection with them now? Notice how brilliant your heart feels. This is singing God's glory: to recognize God's immense compassion and to accept God's love for all people. This is what it means to keep the company of saints and allow the saintliness of others to shine forth in your own heart.

For a moment now, visualize one great quality in yourself that you are pleased with. Perhaps you discovered this great quality on your own, or perhaps it was pointed out to you. Think of one great quality that has supported you, that has radiated from your being. One great quality that has helped others, that has sustained your life. One great quality that has served God. Having visualized this one great quality, remember all the times it brought you happiness. Every time this good quality appeared, how did you feel? Remember all the good things that came about because of this one quality. Remember the gratitude that flowed from your heart when you realized you actually possessed such a wonderful treasure. Understand that the merits of many lifetimes have taken the form of this sterling quality in your being.

To recognize even one good quality within yourself is to sing God's glory. It is to extol God for His kindness. It is to love God for His generosity. It is to sing God's glory for His unconditional acceptance of you. As Brahmananda says:

Don't go searching outside.
The Beloved dwells inside your body.

On the spiritual path, it is meditation that strengthens your perseverance and focuses it in the right direction. When you have a natural propensity toward meditation, it is a sure sign of the blossoming of God's love in your heart. It is a definite signal that enthusiasm for God's universe is coursing through your body. Meditation is the practice that helps you keep the company of your own saintliness. It is like worshiping the rising sun within your own heart. It means giving your undivided attention to the inner music. You become absorbed in the vibration of the mantra that hums throughout your being day and night. In meditation, you actually touch the body of God. Not only do you come in contact with your own great Self, but you receive all that the Self stands for.

Baba Muktananda, in his book *Secret of the Siddhas*, explains what is imparted when a seeker meditates and moves close to the Self, the source of all things. He speaks about *ātmā bala sparsha*, the inspiration coming from contact with the strength of the Self. Through this contact with the supreme Principle, the senses obtain the ability to carry out their work.

*Ātmā bala sparsha* is coming in contact with the power of your own great Self. It is like dipping your mind and heart in a bowl of nectar every second of the day and coming from that space no matter what is happening in your life — good things or bad, pleasant things or unpleasant, joys or sorrows. *Ātmā bala sparsha* means continually maintaining the auspicious state of your mind, which is its true nature. Meditation is like bathing in a holy river all the time. Meditation is one of the best ways to replenish yourself. The senses constantly expend the energy of the body. As they work, the body as a whole becomes depleted, not just the physical body but the subtle body also, which includes the mind, the intellect, the emotions, and the breath.

People often say that they feel they are doing valuable work by helping others, by listening to their problems and giving them time and attention. They say, "I give and I give and I give." But then after a while, they begin to experience a gnawing, haunting emptiness. They feel scorched by the intense heat of the desert created in their minds. Then they say, "I feel as though when I speak to people and listen to their miseries, I lose my soul. I feel so devoid of the Presence within."

Without constantly replenishing yourself from the wellspring of your own heart, you do feel drained. Meditation quenches your deep thirst with a powerful and soothing energy.

Once you recognize the true meaning and value of the power of meditation, then you meditate simply for the joy of it, for the love of it. You don't wonder, "Do I go deep in meditation? Do I have visions? Is my body becoming attuned to the *shakti* or not?" You just sit for meditation. It may be a very ordinary session, it may be quite dramatic. You may feel something, you may not feel anything, but you just sit. When you sit with a child, you just sit there. You don't expect the child to entertain you, to say something sweet or tell you a story so you can feel better. You sit there and everything happens naturally. In the same way, you sit in meditation. Just as you simply breathe, you simply meditate. To be alive in the true sense of the word, you sing God's glory by meditating. And that's why Brahmananda says, "O my dear one, look within."

Baba spoke about his deep love for meditation in his book *Play of Consciousness.* He said, "I did not meditate out of fear, but with enthusiasm and faith and love. I did not meditate to please anyone or to get any benefits from anyone or to satisfy a desire. . . . I did not meditate to rid myself of any illness, physical or mental, nor to gain fame through the miraculous and supernatural powers I might acquire. No one forced me to meditate. . . . I meditated solely for the love of God, because I was irresistibly drawn toward the goddess Chiti Shakti and to explore my own true nature."

When you meditate, the silence of the senses illumines the presence of God within. God emerges in that silence and stands before you. The restfulness of the senses draws the light of God into manifestation. That which is invisible becomes visible. That which is inaudible becomes audible. The quietness of the inner atmosphere reveals the hidden glory of the Divine. The evenness of the inbreath and the outbreath lets the light of the Self shine forth. The fire of meditation purifies your whole inner realm. The strength of meditation holds up the entire universe.

Many great experiences take place during meditation; you don't have to try to force anything. Even if you think nothing is happening, that is really all right because in what you think of as nothingness, something is truly happening. So be filled with enthusiasm and allow your being to bow to God's glory.

Let it be completely comfortable with God. Become totally comfortable with God's energy. It is your own energy.

Enthusiasm dances in every cell of your body. Recognize it. Become quiet and listen to your inner being singing God's glory. Allow yourself to be enveloped in the flames of enthusiasm. Let them inspire each cell of your being. Be determined to maintain the auspicious state of your mind. Let your mind make everything it touches shine forth with divine brilliance. It doesn't matter what thought you have, let it be touched by *ātmā bala sparsha*, the splendor of the Self, the brilliance inherent within the Self.

With great respect, with great love, I welcome you all with all my heart.

*Sadgurunāth mahārāj kī jay!*

*Chapter 3*

# The Wellspring of Enthusiasm

With great respect, with great love, I welcome you all with all my heart.

We are drawing closer to the wellspring of enthusiasm and looking into its inexhaustible nature. Enthusiasm — the fullness of God within, the fullness of God in the heart, the ringing of God's name in the bloodstream. Baba Muktananda always said that the name of God should sing in your bloodstream. He would ask with such enthusiasm, "Does your bloodstream sing the name of God?" And he would answer, "Yes, it does!" You just have to pay attention. Sometimes you hear it as a whisper and sometimes it is much louder than anything else in this world.

Enthusiasm — the glory of God's light and God's energy rising within you, spreading throughout your being. What else can you do but sing His glory? In all your actions, in all your words, in all your thoughts and feelings, be filled with enthusiasm and sing God's glory. Let your bloodstream sing the name of God, let it sing God's glory.

Every particle of the universe is continually revealing its own innate enthusiasm. Each person who contemplates the true meaning of enthusiasm experiences it bubbling up from within. And why not? The heart dances when it comes to know the inner *shakti*. When you realize this ancient power residing within you, of course you are filled with enthusiasm.

Abhinavagupta, a great Siddha of Kashmir, poured the wealth of his spiritual attainment into a magnificent work called the *Tantrāloka*. He situates the wellspring of enthusiasm at the very origin of the universe. The sage says:

> The merging of Shiva and Shakti is the energy of bliss from which the entire universe comes into being, a reality beyond the Supreme and the non-supreme. It is called the Goddess, the essence, and the glorious heart. This is the creation, the supreme Lord.[1]

Who are Shiva and Shakti? Shiva is the formless, all-pervasive, supreme Reality. Shakti is the creative energy of Shiva. She is the Mother who weaves the entire universe of names and forms from Her own being. She projects this entire universe upon Her own screen, and She uses Herself as the material. A potter may use clay to create a pot, but Shakti uses Herself to create this universe. And where does She place this universe? Upon Her own being, not separate from Herself.

This is the true wellspring of enthusiasm, the *ānanda shakti* of Shiva and Shakti, the energy of bliss. For enthusiasm to endure and remain alive, it must be that pure. It must spring directly from its own source, from the great source of Shiva and Shakti. This source is the center of merging, the union of God and His energy, the wellspring of enthusiasm.

How do Shiva and Shakti merge? How is this union possible? Do the ocean and sky merge into each other? Do oil and water merge into each other? Do the mind and the heart merge into each other? Are such things really possible? Anyone who has the power of reasoning will know they are impossible. So does this mean that merging never takes place? Is union just a dream? Does it mean you will never experience the ultimate Truth, the goal of yoga, the state the scriptures describe?

No, it does not mean that. You must not let your God-given enthusiasm dry up just because you cannot find an immediate answer to your questions, or because your reasoning does not arrive at a resolution pleasing to the mind. Just because your intellect is not able to fathom it does not mean the union never takes place.

The sages reveal the answer in their own mystical way. They call merging by another name so you can understand how such union truly takes place. They call it "recognition." The recognition of oneness. That which exists in the ocean also exists in the sky. That which exists in oil also exists in water. That which exists in the mind also exists in the heart. In this act of divine recognition, the illusion of separation dissolves and merging does indeed take place. You will recognize the essence of everything. That which is within you is also within the universe. That which is within the universe is also within you. The wellspring of enthusiasm arises from *ānanda shakti*, the merging of Shiva and Shakti. As Jnaneshwar Maharaj says in his ecstatic book *Amritānubhava*:

> Seated on the same ground,
> wearing the same garment of light,
> they dwell together in eternal bliss.[2]

At the highest level of awareness, one experiences the fullness of merging, the perfection of this union. What keeps a person from experiencing this? Imagine a house that stands on top of a hill and faces east. It's a clear morning at the moment of sunrise. How much light can enter the house? Think about it. Are the curtains drawn or are they open? Is the door open or shut? In the same way, according to your capacity to recognize the essence of everything, you will experience different degrees of merging.

Baba Muktananda describes his Guru's state of union in his sublime book *Secret of the Siddhas*: "O Nityananda, you were perpetually bathed in bliss. Your name itself was bliss. When you laughed, joy and ecstasy burst forth from every pore of your body, as if your skin ripped open with a sudden outrush of your joy."

*Ānanda shakti*, the wellspring of enthusiasm, the recognition of oneness — it comes over you in so many different ways. A great Western poet responds to a moment of intense joy by saying, "Suddenly I realized that if I stepped out of my body I would break into blossom."[3]

The wellspring of enthusiasm. At times you feel so intoxicated, so ecstatic that you are not aware of whether you are walking on the ground or on air. When this happens, just let it happen, let it be. Then there are times when you experience the intense pain of tenderness and a longing so visceral it hurts. You know that everything you aspire to is only a hair's breadth away, yet it seems so far. There are also times when you resist the awareness of the One, the divine Essence in all beings in this entire universe. You are afraid of losing your so-called world, everything you know, the familiar surroundings that most people call normal.

Although the wellspring of enthusiasm is constantly flowing, although *ānanda shakti* is ever fresh, ever giving, you are not always able to drink from it, you are not always willing to accept its grace. Why is this? What is it that keeps a seeker from diving into his own wellspring and experiencing his own bliss?

The yogic texts describe a series of obstacles that block the wellspring of enthusiasm and keep this energy from bubbling up into your awareness. Although these blocks are quite mystical by nature, they shed a great deal of light on the human condition. Haven't you noticed that certain habits completely dry up your enthusiasm for life, for sadhana, for your spiritual practices? Habits like criticizing yourself and other people, being defensive when your faults are pointed out, or even worse, apathetic. Then there is malice. Lack of restraint. Impatience. Hypocrisy. Cruelty. How can enthusiasm penetrate these qualities? What else weighs you down? Doubts eat away at enthusiasm, as does unfriendliness. Also, haughtiness.

Disrespect. Hurting others. Speaking caustic words. Showing constant dissatisfaction. All these qualities are the by-products, the offspring, of these blocks, and they are the enemies of enthusiasm.

What are these blocks? Where do they come from? The yogic texts call them the *granthis*, the knots. There are three main *granthis*, and they cause a person to be contracted, to be bound in limited ideas. Because of these knots, a person lives in a finite world of appearances where everything is perishable. As Vedanta would say, you consider that which is perishable to be imperishable, and therefore you constantly experience sorrow. The *granthis* fool people into thinking they understand the world, when in fact they are basing all their judgments on appearances, on the effects only, without ever understanding the cause. These *granthis* keep a person revolving in his or her own self-created world of delusions. So when you ask what is it that keeps a person from experiencing his own *ānanda shakti*, the source of enthusiasm within him, the answer is the *granthis*, the knots that impede the rise of *kundalinī* to the state of union.

In time, through the grace of the Guru, these knots are released. It happens gradually, subtly but steadily, all through your sadhana. Often you are not aware of it, but it is an ongoing miracle nevertheless. When the three knots are finally undone, they help you to have divine experiences. The very obstacles that held you back are transmuted and now reveal the true nature of the great Self.

These *granthis* are located in the subtle body, an energy body that interpenetrates the physical body and gives it vitality. The first knot is called the *brahmā granthi* and it is found at the base of the spine in the *mūlādhāra chakra*. Brahma represents the creator. As long as the *shakti* is blocked in this area, a person cannot experience true enthusiasm. He lives, but he is only going through the motions of life. He passes through life as a beast does, without recognizing his own inherent divinity. Remember, the enthusiasm that we want to discover is not an occasional emotional outburst, such as one might experience when a lifelong wish comes true. This enthusiasm is a deep, unbroken connection to the bliss of the Absolute. When the energy is blocked at the *brahmā granthi*, a person sees, but always with a sense that there is a wall in front of him, always with a sense of separation. The seer and the seen remain separate. There is no recognition of the essence in either of them.

The second knot is the *vishnu granthi*, and it is located in the *anāhata chakra*, the heart center. This *granthi* is also called the knot of the heart. When the energy is blocked here, all the auspicious qualities, all the great virtues, are obscured. There is no sign of generosity, tenderness, harmony, sacredness, nobility, reverence, divine beauty, devotion, kindness, sweetness, magnificence, or good fortune. Therefore, a person goes about his day feeling that his heart is closed tight. He feels deprived of life energy. Just as when you don't eat food for a while, the physical body experiences deprivation, in the same way, the heart experiences the deprivation of these auspicious and sacred qualities. Such a person feels that nothing in this world can bring any kind of happiness. He experiences gloominess most of the time and finds no *rasa* in living, no juiciness, no flavor, no zest. Constant criticism of the universe becomes his sacred text. And of course, with all the auspiciousness removed from the world of his heart, he ends up looking like a withered flower. The sap of life runs murky in his veins.

Lord Vishnu represents the power that sustains and supports whatever has been brought into manifestation. In the same way, on a subtle level it is the heart that must sustain the loveliness of life, the divinity within. However, when the heart is obstructed, it becomes listless and cannot maintain its own dharma; it cannot perform its sacred function. So the very center that should be shining and lovely, shimmering with golden rays, is darkened by a terrible *granthi*, by a knot, the *vishnu granthi*.

The third knot in the subtle body is called the *rudra granthi.* It is located in the *ājñā chakra*, in the space between the eyebrows. This is a crucial center through which the awakened *shakti* must pass. When it is blocked, a person cannot see beyond his illusions. It is as though a heavy lid has closed upon him. Such people feel as though they are constantly carrying a huge weight as they walk, as they eat, as they drink, as they go to sleep, as they perform their actions. Even if they are having wonderful thoughts, they cannot feel lightness, lightheartedness. They never feel they themselves could fly. When this *granthi* is blocked, a person experiences a lack of everything in his or her life. He simply cannot step into a greater awareness, an expanded vision. No matter how much such people receive, they never feel they are receiving anything. Although such a person may know she is uncomfortable, she never knows why. She can't see her way out. She thinks that's just how life is. Such people say, "Well, after all, I'm just a human being."

When I hear people say such things, I am reminded of the poems of great beings who speak about the value of human life. In this human birth you can know God, you can recognize the Truth. So when you say, "Well, I'm just a human being. I've got my faults. What can I do?" you should think about it. A human being is truly great. Thank your good fortune that you *are* a human being! In this human life you can experience the radiance of God. In this human body you can accomplish so much. However, because of this particular *granthi*, you experience such limitations.

This third *granthi* is named after Rudra, a form of Lord Shiva. Rudra represents the power of dissolution, which symbolizes not destruction per se, but giving way to a greater manifestation, dissolving that which is unnecessary and giving birth to divinity. However, this transformation is not possible as long as the knot of Rudra blocks the passageway to unity awareness, to the merging of Shiva and Shakti. How can this block be pierced? In his book *Kundalini: The Secret of Life*, Baba Muktananda says:

"There is a knot in the *sushumnā*, within the cranial region, called the *rudra granthi*, or knot of Rudra. This knot is opened by the tip of the tongue as it touches it during *khecharī mudrā*."

*Khecharī mudrā* is a spontaneous movement of the tongue. During meditation it curls back against the palate and moves upward. This movement takes place without your effort. Sometimes when newcomers experience *khecharī mudrā* after receiving *shaktipāt* in the Intensive, they may become frightened. They can't believe that their tongue can suddenly become so long and perform such unfamiliar gymnastics inside their familiar mouth. However, Baba explains that once this spontaneous movement occurs, "the awakened Shakti rises to the *sahasrāra*, to unite with Shiva dwelling there. After this, one starts to experience *samādhi* states and taste the divine nectar."

The sages describe these blocks in a very mystical way. A great deal goes on as they dissolve. You must understand one thing clearly: these knots cannot be released through self-effort alone. The *granthis* have been in this form for ages. It takes a very powerful force to pierce them. They can be broken only by the incredible power of the awakened Kundalini and the Guru's grace.

The *Shiva Samhitā*, a storehouse of esoteric knowledge about Kundalini and Her workings, says:

> When the sleeping goddess Kundalini is awakened through the Guru's grace, then all the chakras and knots are pierced.[4]

As long as Kundalini Shakti is asleep, the *ānanda shakti*, the wellspring of enthusiasm, is also dormant. You have no access to it. You may have glimpses of your own enthusiasm, but you are not able to drink it at will. In that case, a person may think he is enjoying sense pleasures, but truly speaking, his experiences are like tiny droplets of water that evaporate as quickly as they land on the palm of the hand. Such pleasures vanish almost before they are enjoyed. They do not endure, nor do they take a seeker in the right direction. They are born out of *māyā*, the power of illusion.

As long as the *granthis* are blocked, the experience of bliss is also hidden away. At the moment of *shaktipāt*, the Guru transmits his own fully awakened energy into a disciple. This awakens Kundalini where She lies sleeping at the base of the spine. The Goddess begins to stir. In Her upward movement, the *granthis* are pierced. In some people this happens dramatically, and all of the *granthis* open right away with a great rush of energy. In other people it happens slowly and gradually. Whichever way it happens, quickly or little by little, be grateful — it is a divine process.

When these *granthis* or knots become undone, you do experience discomfort in the body. Sometimes you feel feverish. At other times the body moves, either gently or very forcefully. Sometimes you may have an outburst of feeling and you don't know where it has come from. Memories and impressions may come to the surface. Therefore people consider themselves fortunate when the *granthis* undo themselves slowly and gradually. Then they can actually enjoy the process. If the *granthis* undo themselves rapidly, you may find yourself thinking, "I can't wait for this one to finish. I can't wait to get over this one." Whichever way it happens for you, just enjoy each moment as it unfolds. When these knots are being pierced, a purifying process is taking place. Accept it and welcome it with great wonder. This process draws you closer to the wellspring of enthusiasm, and you are able to experience your own bliss.

The source of enthusiasm lies within everyone. It is within reach. You can actually find it and drink its endless wisdom, its divine freshness, its life energy. It is continually flowing and full of bliss. To experience this wellspring, to keep it fresh and replenished, you must draw from it constantly. The more you draw from this inner source, the more abundant it becomes. And the opposite is just as true. When you stop turning to the wellspring, when you neglect it, it recedes farther and farther from reach. It becomes like an abandoned village well that no longer gives fresh clear water.

Perhaps you have seen what happens when a village well is abandoned. When people stop coming first thing in the morning and again at dusk to lift fresh clear water from its cool shadowy depths. When no one comes to quench his thirst or draw water to take home for drinking or cooking. What happens when no one comes to the well? Does the water stay fresh? Yes, for a while. There is a period of continued serenity and purity — until the first accident. Maybe a branch falls into the water and is not removed, or maybe someone walking by wants to get rid of some trash and carelessly tosses it in the well. There is always a beginning, a first step in a downfall, and it is usually quite ordinary, not at all dramatic.

But once deterioration sets in, it has a way of accelerating. If the tree limb is left in the water, it rots and makes the well brackish. If dust and leaves are left to collect on the surface of the water, they congeal. Then mosquitoes breed. Disease festers. Naturally, people will begin to dump their trash around a well like that. Eventually, hoodlums move into the area. You would never dream of drinking water from such a well. You would go out of your way to avoid it.

Of course you might ask, why would people abandon such an excellent well in the first place? There might be all kinds of reasons. Someone may have said that there was better water in another place. Perhaps someone dug another well in a more convenient location. Or perhaps in a hot spell people feared the well would run dry and they got out of the habit of using it. Or some neighbors might have quarreled and begun avoiding the common source of water for reasons they might have even forgotten in time. Maybe vandals cut the rope and stole the bucket so many times that people got tired of replacing it.

Or maybe rumors started: someone got sick and blamed the water; someone was robbed there very early in the morning. Or perhaps someone saw a ghost. The possibilities are endless. But when you come right down to it, whatever the reason was, the result is neglect. And the unfortunate truth is, once it starts, neglect triggers a process of decline that develops its own momentum and is very difficult to stop.

We are talking about ancient wells and villages, but truly speaking, the analogy is not so distant. Take a moment now and ask yourself: How many times have I abandoned my own wellspring of enthusiasm, my own source of joy, clarity, purity, and refreshment? Did I ever turn away from the immaculate fountain of peace inside myself? If I did, why? Did I let myself become distracted by easy pleasures even if they soon dried up? Did I gradually become accustomed to another source of water, one that was less clear, less pure, until I actually forgot the taste of the real thing? Or was I afraid of going deeper within? Afraid of unknown predators that might be lurking inside me: shameful memories, pain or guilt, ghosts from the past? Or was it something on the outside that lured me away? Did I get a little bit lazy perhaps and look around for a well that was easier to maintain? How did I abandon my wellspring of enthusiasm? What stops me from going within?

You have so much worthiness. The wellspring of enthusiasm, the unending source of your joy, lies within you. You must draw upon it over and over again. By doing this, you are not inflating your ego; you are not becoming arrogant or conceited. Actually, you are showing appreciation for God and what He has put inside you, for the gifts He has given you, for all the resources you have received.

Within you is the Master, the great power of Kundalini. Let Her dissolve the inner *granthis*, the knots that block the unfolding of your heart's energy. When the inner knots are released, when the *granthis* are broken, the life energy flows, the drought is over. You experience a river of freshness and joy that wholly absorbs your mind and senses. It is as if nothing else exists in this world — just this life energy. Only this indescribable purity, clarity, delight. The taste is ambrosia. The feeling of abundance is endless.

As you pursue your spiritual practices and continue to experience and explore your own innate enthusiasm, you are treading the same path that the knowers of the Truth have followed. Each of the great beings describes what he or she finds in a manner that is unique, mystical, crystal clear, and poetic. The unmistakable force of their experience comes through their teachings and songs.

One of India's poet-saints says:

> Enraptured, one descends into the inner realms
> and goes deep into intense meditation.
> In this state, the world is soon forgotten,
> and there remains only the recognition of the unstruck sound.[5]
> In the depths of my being I met Brahman, the Absolute,
> as if Consciousness had entered into me.
> That inner resting place has no attributes.
> It is radiant. It is a space not easily known.
>
> The inner moon has a luster
> a thousand times greater than that of the external moon.
> The inner sun is indescribably brilliant.
> I see a radiant place within myself.
> So exquisite is its beauty
>     that I faint while marveling at it.
>
> There is a shower of lightning, a mine of diamonds.
> That space is beyond all sorrows;
>     it is farther than the farthest.
> It is unique in all the worlds.

The lotus opened, and the boon was granted.
Now I drink the inner nectar day and night,
and I eat the celestial fruit
    that destroys sin and drives away delusion.

I have given up praising or criticizing others.
This is what happens in the state of liberation.
When you understand the supreme Principle,
there is no more pleasure or sorrow.

The five elements and twenty-five principles of creation
    have left me.
I have won the field.[6]
I have understood beyond a trace of doubt
    that my *sadguru* is my only love.[7]

Another lover of God sings, "How intoxicated are they who have achieved the state of inner liberation." When you experience the divinity in your own being, you realize that great intoxication exists within you.

As you experience this intoxication, the life energy bubbling up from the wellspring of enthusiasm, you are able to see everything very clearly. Colors become brighter when you open up from within, and the words you hear from others are filled with sweetness. You have so many great inner resources.

The wellspring of enthusiasm is your birthright. It is the whole purpose of your coming to this world. Constantly draw from this wellspring: you will experience your own divinity, your own immense treasure.

With great respect, with great love, I welcome you all with all my heart.

*Sadgurunāth mahārāj kī jay!*

Chapter 4

# The True Companion Within

With great respect, with great love, I welcome you all with all my heart.

For some time now we have been contemplating the message "Be filled with enthusiasm and sing God's glory." How swiftly this wondrous time has rolled back into the infinite folds of eternity. No matter how great your intention may be to imbibe the meaning of these words and put it into practice, you always wish you had more time. You want to investigate the depths and dimensions of this teaching, to really feel its texture and make it your own. You want to explore this treasure and let it transform you completely.

Exactly how does one go about diving into a message like this? In a sacred text called the *Ātmabodha*, the great sage Shankaracharya addressed this question over a thousand years ago:

> When a seeker hears the Truth and contemplates it,
> the fire of knowledge is kindled within.
> Then, freed from impurities, he shines like gold.[1]

The teachings that you hear from the great ones and the scriptures ignite a beneficial fire within. This fire is beneficial because of what it begins to burn away: painful thoughts, unresolved feelings, dampening emotions, and the old tenacious grudges you have kept stored in the attic of your mind, the trunks and trunks of misconceptions you have been lugging around for years. It is the Truth blazing in the teachings that reduces your useless tendencies to ashes. The teachings burn away impurities. As you apply yourself to the practices of yoga, the teachings come alive for you. Your understanding deepens and actually becomes your experience, which is ever increasing, ever new. You constantly feel you are uncovering a new "you." Sometimes you may recognize this very quickly; sometimes it may require an inner adjustment.

The more you contemplate the teachings, the more they enter you. You examine their worth attentively and you try to apply them. Increasingly, you see the impact of the teachings on your life. You come to understand their incredible power, which enables you to uphold dharma, to live a life of goodness. You realize how timely these timeless messages are for you, right now. And you begin to surrender to your own inner Self. This is what the teachings give you: they give you the power to surrender to your Self again and again. When that happens, these beautiful, fruitful teachings begin to arise from within of their own accord. Having heard them over and over again in the scriptures, in satsangs, from fellow seekers, you let them anoint your being. And then, as the *Ātmabodha* says, you shine like gold.

The sages are so great. Listen to the teachings, they say; contemplate them; imbibe them; put them into practice; and then you will shine like gold. They don't say, if you put the teachings into practice then the scriptures will become greater, or then the sages will be considered such wonderful beings, or then you will truly be making God shine in this world. No. They say *you* will shine like gold. They always bring it back to your own great Self.

The kind of life you lead when you follow the teachings, when you become aware of God's presence in your heart, is truly golden. You no longer live an ordinary life, you live a golden life. You live yoga. You are not just marking off the days, the weeks, the months. Each day becomes a beautiful garland of your contemplations and reflections, your unselfish deeds, profound transformations, fruitful actions, meditations, chanting, kind thoughts, loving vibrations, enlightening revelations, and purposeful living. At the end of the day, you offer this garland to the great Lord whose glory your heart sings without ceasing. But it doesn't end there. Everything that happens in the night also becomes an offering to the Lord. Each day and each night becomes another exquisite garland for you to offer. This is what the spiritual path holds for you.

The teachings of the sages are penetrating. Take them in. They are valuable. Even if you are able to grasp only a minuscule portion of what you hear or read, allow your heart to embrace it. Allow the teachings to penetrate your being. It doesn't matter if you are hearing a teaching for the first time or for the thousandth time, allow it to reveal a newer, greater meaning. Let it enter you. Then that tiny ray will expand, and your intellect will be illumined by its radiance.

There was once a simple peasant, a good-hearted seeker named Bhai Bella, who came to the Guru looking for initiation. The Guru received him and sent him to the stables to tend the horses. "Look after them well," he instructed. "Groom them carefully and take good care of them."

Now Bhai Bella was not well educated, he was not well read at all, but he knew the worth of the Guru's words. He fed the horses on time, groomed them, exercised them, nursed their sores, and cleaned the stables until they shone. He loved serving in the stables. And within a few months, all the horses were healthier and happier than they had ever been before.

The Guru was very pleased, and one day he called for the disciple and said, "Bhai Bella, I see you are now ready to learn the scriptures." From then on, every morning the Guru would give him an aphorism from one of the scriptures. Bhai Bella would hear it, contemplate it, and let it seep into his entire being. He absorbed every letter of the aphorism, every curve of every letter. He continued to work in the stables and serve the horses. And bit by bit, his understanding grew.

One morning the Guru had to leave quite early, and he was in a hurry. When he came to the stable for his horse, Bhai Bella stopped him and asked, "O Master, what about my teaching for the day? O Gurudev, please initiate me into a new aphorism." And he bowed humbly.

The Guru looked at him and said, "Bhai Bella, you do not recognize the proper time or the appropriate place. Go!" This made Bhai Bella very happy and he immediately began to repeat the *sūtra* he had received from the Guru. "Bhai Bella, you do not recognize the proper time or the appropriate place. Go!" All day long as he worked with the horses, he repeated it, he sang it. He became completely intoxicated.

All the other students in the ashram, who were intelligent, well educated, and sophisticated, began to talk about Bhai Bella. "Bhai Bella doesn't understand the difference between the Guru's critical remarks and a *sūtra* from the scriptures. He's such a simpleton, so naive, a village bumpkin." They made fun of him and called him names as he walked by. "What a fool. He would have to stay here a thousand years before he could understand anything."

But Bhai Bella remained in his state of intoxication, repeating his Guru's words: "Bhai Bella, you do not recognize the proper time or the appropriate place. Go!" His entire being was tingling; it was filled with beautiful vibrations. As soon as the Guru returned to the ashram, all the students ran to him, saying, "O Guruji, Bhai Bella has really lost his mind. He has gone crazy! You should see him!" The Guru listened to their reports and then said, "Call for Bhai Bella."

They found Bhai Bella sitting under a tree, swaying and chanting the Guru's remark. They shook him and said, "Bhai Bella! Bhai Bella! Guruji wants to see you. Come quickly." Bhai Bella stood up to go, but he was so intoxicated, he could hardly walk. As he approached and bowed, the Guru immediately saw Bhai Bella's state. His entire face had changed. His whole being was vibrating with the knowledge of the scriptures. The Guru looked straight into his eyes and said, "Bhai Bella has attained everything."

When Bhai Bella heard the Guru's words, he became completely steady within. He was anchored in the knowledge of the Self. It was as though the purest being was emerging from him.

As the days went by, it was very clear that Bhai Bella had attained everything. When he was working in the stable, the work seemed to happen of its own accord: he didn't have to do much at all. Just by his being there, the right things took place. The horses were more and more docile, and they would greet Bhai Bella as he approached. In fact, he would hear the words of the Guru coming out of the horses. If he sat by one of the ashram walls, he would hear the Guru's words coming from the walls. He would hear the teachings in the running water of a nearby stream. Wherever he looked, he would see the Guru's face and hear the Guru's teachings.

It became very clear to all the other students that the Guru had, in fact, given Bhai Bella the greatest attainment. And they were jealous. They went to the Guru and complained, "O Guruji, why? We've been in your ashram for so many years. Bhai Bella is very new. He came to the ashram just a year ago, and already he has received everything. Why are you so partial, so unkind? Why haven't you given the same thing to us?"

The Guru said, "You are like a patient who receives medicine from the doctor and just rinses his mouth with it and spits it out instead of swallowing it. How can such a patient be cured? When Bhai Bella listens to the teachings, he drinks them in with vigilance and devotion. Each word has entered Bhai Bella and kindled the fire of wisdom."

Allow the teachings to penetrate your being. Let them enter you. A teaching may come from a little child; it may come from a tree or a stream. It may come in a dream. You may experience great knowledge arising from within when you are talking with a friend, studying with a scholar, or just staring into space. However it comes, receive it as a most precious boon. Be filled with enthusiasm and sing God's glory.

In the *Bhagavad Gītā*, Lord Krishna tells his disciple, Arjuna:

> Truly, nothing in this world purifies like knowledge. He who in time becomes perfect in yoga finds this knowledge in his own Self.[2]

Knowledge of the Self arises from within. As you walk the spiritual path, knowledge of the Self becomes your true companion. It stands by you. Whatever happens, whether you are joyful or sorrowful, whether you are making progress or being challenged by adversity, knowledge of the Self supports you. It steadies you and lights your way.

You can think of it this way: when your body is healthy and strong and all your physical limbs are intact, when your senses and nerves are functioning impeccably, you have a lot of energy. And you expend it in a breathtaking variety of ways: You rush about. You climb mountains. You create hundreds of computer programs. You wrestle. You travel at lightning speed. You give highly motivating, energetic, powerful, and compelling speeches. You cook special meals and please all your loved ones. You go to weddings and parties. You work until the early hours of the morning. You go horseback riding or parachuting from airplanes. You start campaigns and fight for causes. You keep yourself incredibly busy for a hundred different reasons. Your body is healthy, you feel so strong, you have so much energy — you must do something!

You are motivated by all sorts of things: A desire for name and fame. A need to fight off emotions or to fill up your time. An urge to look important or to make yourself feel inferior (people do work hard at that, you know). You are motivated by an interest in making yourself happy or you simply need to have something to do. But mainly you are willing to go to any extreme as long as you don't have to be alone with yourself. That old, ancient loneliness is what you want to avoid. Anything to get away from the deafening silence that resounds within, from your pure conscience that always speaks the truth. And so over time, the inevitable happens. You lose touch with your own immaculate heart that shines with God's light. You lose contact with the loving energy that would guide you on the right path.

Have you ever seriously thought about the other side of the equation? What happens when your limbs lose the power to run around? When you are physically incapacitated and cannot move a millimeter? At a time like this, how do you manage? When your mind is still intact but the rest of you is atrophying, when you are toxic with the poison of boredom, how do you battle with your own unending restlessness? Your unfulfilled desires? The uselessness of your days? The burden of your existence on others? How do you rise to the continuous challenge of quieting your desperate thoughts, your sinking willpower, your unbearable dejection? How do you fill the nights that seem to go on forever?

Where do you take refuge at a time like this when your body is no longer healthy, when it cannot move? When you have lost all the physical strength you thought you could use to win over the world? You long to find a resting place, a little peace and quiet. Where does such a place exist? And if it does exist, how do you go about finding it when you can't even move? You can't travel to a holy place. You can't visit your friends. You can't even pick up the telephone to call someone and say you are dying.

How long can you curse your destiny? Who is there to blame? Whom do you call for? Who will listen? And in the final analysis, who can do anything that will help? Where is your refuge? Who is your refuge?

In one incisive song after another, the Indian saints throughout history have sent out the warning: death is laughing at you. They say, when you think you are busy with so many activities, when you think you are so important, pay attention:

death is laughing at you. The poet-saint Tulsidas sings:

> It's as if you thought your body was shielded with copper
>     and you didn't need the Lord.
> But don't you know that death is hovering overhead?
>
> Who hasn't surrounded himself with land and house,
>     wife and wealth, children and friends?
> But do they belong to you?
> Can they go with you when you go?
>
> Kings who thought they ruled the entire world,
>     where are they today?
> What became of those kings?
> Death ate them for breakfast.[3]
> What then will he do with you and me?[4]

Another lover of God sings:

> You saunter around in the garden
> like a dandy with a flower in your turban.
> One blow of death
> and you will forget all your gaiety in a moment.[5]

Kabir, the great saint and mystic of Benares, says:

> It is idle fantasy to say
> that your soul will automatically merge in God when you die.
> If the Lord is found now,
> He is also found then.
> If you don't make an effort to know Him now,
> then you will simply end up with an apartment in
>     the City of Death.[6]

Please don't think that the saints sing these verses to be pessimistic. Don't even entertain the idea that they want to depress you. They just want to make everyone aware of the ultimate helplessness of the physical body.

I heard an anecdote recently from the mother of a seven-year-old. The young girl was talking on the phone with a friend, and after she hung up, she began to laugh and laugh.

"Mom," she said, "you won't believe what my friend said! I asked him, 'Would you like to come and play with me today?' And he said, 'Yes, I do want to do something today, but not with my body.'"

The little girl was laughing really hard. "Mom, can you believe he wants to do something but not with his body?" When I heard that story, I had been contemplating these verses about the physical body and I thought, "There is wisdom everywhere."

This message that the saints give is very piercing. They want to take you beyond the bondage of the physical body. They want you to realize that the body is as transitory as a butterfly's wings and that the happiness you find in it is just as short-lived. Become aware that there is a greater happiness, they say. The wisdom of the Self, the light of God within — that is your true companion. When everything works, when nothing works, the knowledge of the Self keeps you anchored; it keeps you afloat. Welcome the teachings wholeheartedly and generously. Give yourself to the practices as you never have before. Embrace your true companion within.

After taking part in a Siddha Yoga Meditation Intensive in London, a man was speaking to a friend. He said, "I was a newcomer at the Intensive. I really didn't know what to expect. However, while I was there, I met an old friend of mine."

"Who was it?" asked his companion.

"It was me!" said the man. "I found *myself*, and I knew it was the old friend I had been looking for all my life. During the whole Intensive, I was with this old friend. I was basking in the radiance of the great Self."

If you are looking for something or someone, find this great friend within yourself — your true companion, your wisdom, your knowledge. Allow your inner being to blossom and reveal its glory. Have you ever seen rain falling on parched ground?

Isn't it amazing how quickly the tender green shoots push their way to the surface? It can happen in the twinkling of an eye. Think of the grace of the teachings in the same way — as the sweetest rain falling from heaven. This shower of grace falls upon each moment of your life. Each moment is saturated with the wisdom of the teachings. Allow yourself to be soaked in this wisdom. Let the refreshing knowledge of the Self rise from the core of your being and bring forth its fruit. Truly the core of your being is so strong, so courageous. It is stronger than steel, more radiant than gold. So reach the core of your being. Don't get stuck at the different layers of skin, muscles, and tissues; don't become enmeshed in the different strata of emotions and feelings. Keep traveling deeper and deeper within. Reach the strong core of your being, where you abide all the time. Embrace your true companion within.

Often when people are sad, they say, "Please give me a hug; it will make me feel so good." Or when they meet someone they haven't seen for a long time, they say, "It's so good to see you!" and the two of them embrace. In the same way, embrace your own wisdom, your own true companion. As the tiniest knowledge arises within you, appreciate it, relish it, love being with it. Have respect for this body that contains such wisdom and reveals it at the right time in the right place. Inhale the fragrance of your own wisdom. Take in its pure essence. Hear its sacred message. Embrace its divine possibilities. Taste its sweet nectar. Let it reveal its secrets to you—its depth, its strength, its delicacy, its courage. Make this knowledge your lifelong companion.

Allow each moment of your day to become the embodiment of the Truth. Always remember that each person carries the golden light of the teachings. Let each object shimmer with God's message. Let each element of nature reveal God's magnificence, God's compassion, God's generosity, God's love, the Guru's unconditional love, the ecstasy of the heart. Be with God as He creates the days and nights and suffuses them with His splendor. Be filled with enthusiasm and sing God's glory.

The great sage of Kashmir Shaivism, Abhinavagupta, describes an invaluable step in making this knowledge your lifelong companion. He says:

> The essence of Consciousness is freedom, and the essence of freedom is a mass of bliss, *ānanda*. So in order to attain a state of identity with and absorption in Consciousness, the ritual actions that are performed should employ elements that bring joy to the heart.[7]

This is a beautiful teaching. To cultivate and maintain enthusiasm, you must perform actions that will bring joy to the heart. Enthusiasm itself is the fruit of enthusiasm. It is also a worthy offering to lay before the Lord. There are many, many spiritual practices that enable you to bond with the inner companion: meditation, chanting, mantra repetition, offering selfless service, worship, prayer, contemplation, satsang. Whatever practices give joy to the heart are the rituals you must perform to experience your true companion. These are the practices that enhance the joy of the heart.

The enthusiasm that we are exploring here is not just a single burst of energy, like holiday fireworks. It is not something that expends its whole existence in one magnificent fiery display that takes your breath away. What we are talking about is the enthusiasm that continues to unfold and takes you to the core of your being where your strength, your courage, your God, your love, your gratitude abide. This enthusiasm never diminishes. It is always there — when you are happy and unhappy, when you are joyful and sorrowful, when you are feeling good, and when you are feeling bad. It never diminishes. It continually unfolds itself.

Shaivism says that the essence of Consciousness is freedom, and the essence of that is a mass of bliss. Consciousness is an ever-continuing energy of enthusiasm. Enthusiasm vibrates within it. So this enthusiasm is not a mere show of superficial niceness or formality. Consciousness is not enthusiastic in order to please someone. It is not devoid of intelligence either. Enthusiasm doesn't mean taking a reckless nosedive into something unknown. Quite the opposite. Enthusiasm is an awakened state. It doesn't look for a superficial smile, nor does it look for recognition from others. Enthusiasm is supremely content within itself.

The great Indian poet-saint Jnaneshwar Maharaj was a being who pulsated with divine bliss and enthusiasm. He inspires all those who come in contact with his words and teachings. He says:

> I will make the whole world happy.
> I will lead my life in this world with great joy and love,
> and show everyone that the three worlds
> are really full to overflowing with bliss.
>
> I will go to Pandharpur, the holy place of Consciousness within,
> and there I will meet my true Mother, my true Protector.
>
> I will attain the fruits of all good actions
> when I embrace the Lord within my own heart.
>
> Those devotees who went to meet my Lord within,
> He made them like Himself.
> I will lead my life in this world with great joy and with
> great love,
> and show everyone that the three worlds
> are really full to overflowing with bliss.[8]

Seize the opportunity to discover boundless enthusiasm. Let the practices of yoga unfold miraculous experiences for you. Let them reveal to you how you may spend your days and nights in delight with the inner companion, the knowledge of your astonishingly blissful, divine Self. Let the teachings kindle a fire within that makes you shine like gold. Embrace the true companion within, the knowledge of your own Self, the wisdom of your own Self. Be filled with enthusiasm and sing God's glory.

With great respect, with great love, I welcome you all with all my heart.

*Sadgurunāth mahārāj kī jay!*

*Chapter 5*

# Freedom of Speech

With great respect, with great love, I welcome you all with all my heart.

Each day is filled with opportunities to nourish the incredible fire of enthusiasm. Each moment is blessed with revealing insights to contemplate. Each action can reveal the presence of God's glory within us and all around us. The fire of enthusiasm and the yearning to experience the Truth reveal the deep freedom that each seeker can attain.

Everyone cherishes and respects freedom. When it is put to good use, it brings out the best in a human being. However, people often forget the true purpose of freedom. They seek it everywhere, yet when it finally arrives in their life, they rarely know how to live with it.

Among the many freedoms people cherish, freedom of speech ranks high. Freedom of speech is a valuable privilege, a precious gift, yet people often forget that with it comes an awesome responsibility.

The Indian scriptures hold the faculty of speech in great esteem. To speak beautifully, sweetly, eloquently, kindly, lovingly, you invoke the goddess of speech, Saraswati. She is the divine power that flows through syllables, and she is also the embodiment of goodness. In fact, you always see her in pictures wearing a white garment, the garment of light, purity, and goodness. Words that flow as lucidly as clear water, words that sound as sweet as the fragrance of flowers are her gifts.

Saraswati is the embodiment of knowledge, the inspirer of wisdom. Words that are uttered with her blessings create beauty in the hearts of speakers as well as listeners. For this reason, in India every student is taught to offer obeisance to her before beginning any kind of study, whether it is secular or religious.

With the blessings of Saraswati, speech is pure, speech is true, speech is uplifting, speech opens the heart and warms the soul, speech brings people together and draws them closer to the Self. This is true freedom of speech, the speech that brings us closer to God, that gives us the experience of God's bounty, that allows us to live in this beautiful universe while offering our gratitude to God.

Freedom is a rich subject to contemplate, and it is helpful at the outset to think about how human beings interpret and misinterpret the word. People commonly think that freedom means having free rein to indulge in the ego's appetites. Too often, freedom is sought for the fulfillment of the insatiable desires of the ego. And in the process, the awareness of the highest good falls into neglect. In this headlong rush toward gratification of the ego's appetites, it is easy to forget the virtues that make life worth living: self-restraint, moderation, and consideration for the good of others. It is easy to forget what will benefit society as a whole. The fact that God's hand is in everything somehow slips one's mind, and the right kind of discrimination just disappears. The ability to distinguish short-term pleasures from enduring happiness — this awareness evaporates. And then, even when you get what is most beneficial for you, you don't realize it. You don't understand what you have received. You are unable to recognize its imperishable value. It slips right by you.

Once there was a master alchemist, who knew how to turn base metal into gold. However, he lived very simply and never took advantage of this skill for personal benefit. As his fame spread, many aspirants gathered around him. In particular, there were two aspirants who really wanted to learn what he had to teach. No science can be mastered instantly; you have to live with the master for some time to imbibe the teachings. So these two students went to live with the master alchemist.

One day the alchemist asked them to make the midday meal. They were to stir the grain in an iron wok. The two students were quite happy to serve him in any way because they knew that once the master was pleased with them, he would give them the teachings, he would show them how to turn base metal into gold. So with great delight, they took the special stirring stick and stirred the pot. After a while, they noticed that something extraordinary was happening to the iron wok. It was turning into gold!

Their eyes became bigger and brighter, and their hearts began to flutter. "At last! Here is the wisdom!" they thought. "We've been serving the master for years. He's taken a long time to impart the teaching. This is our time!" Quickly they grabbed some towels and picked up the golden wok. They dropped the stirring stick into the fire and poured the grain into the fire as well. They looked around — but the master alchemist was nowhere to be seen. Throwing a shawl over the golden wok, they headed for the open door and ran far away.

The master alchemist returned to the kitchen. The students were gone. The fire was still blazing high, burning up the grain. And he saw the stick — the alchemist's stick that turns base metal into gold — sitting in the fire. He knew exactly what had happened. He picked up the stick, stroked it, and said, "Ahh, you stay with the master."

In the same way, in the name of exercising freedom, of experiencing freedom, an individual often becomes blind to what gives value to his life, blind to the virtues that are concealed within himself — virtues that the whole world deserves and needs. In the Indian scriptures, freedom of speech is understood on the deepest possible level. It is when the scriptures are recited with reverence that they come to life. It is when mantras are chanted that you are able to experience their great power. It is when wisdom is uttered that it makes itself known. It becomes *sākshāt*, it becomes manifest. A brahmin priest learns to memorize the sacred syllables of the Vedas and imbibes their profound teaching by constant utterance, constant repetition. All this is the domain of Saraswati, the beautiful goddess of speech. In fact, when someone speaks eloquently, sweetly, and with dignity, people in India say, "Oh, the goddess Saraswati is dancing on his tongue. The goddess Saraswati is so pleased with this person."

In this context, then, freedom of speech is not a right that you exercise. Freedom is a state that pure speech engenders inside you. Never take it for granted. Pure speech creates such a beautiful environment within yourself. It is the way we keep the intricate, unique goodness of every culture alive — through stories, folk songs, parables, poetry, drama, and so on. It is one of the foremost ways we communicate God's love to one another.

Freedom of speech is a divinely human attribute. However, when it is abused, when it is made to serve your every whim and mood, it can no longer fulfill its innate purpose. The goddess Saraswati turns away. And what is the result? It is like taking a cupful of sweet nectar, mixing it with poison, and then giving it to everyone you meet. Of course, there is always more than enough to go around. Impulsive, uncontrolled speech may seem attractive in the beginning — in fact, very attractive in the beginning — but the end result is dreadful. Saying whatever you feel like is, in a way, like digging your own grave, like sliding into the jaws of death, the death of morality, the death of harmony, the death of a pure conscience. When you say whatever you feel like saying from one minute to the next, you drown out the quiet voice of God's will.

In the Book of Proverbs, it is said:

> When the words are many, transgression is not lacking.
> But he who restrains his lips is prudent.[1]

Have you ever noticed what happens when you go on talking and talking? Gradually, almost without realizing it, you vacate the realm of restraint. Have you had that experience? When you keep talking endlessly, you start out by spilling all kinds of things that have been so significant to you, but you end up tarnishing other people's reputations. Usually you say more than you meant to. You give reality to things you may not even mean.

Then, when you walk away from such a conversation, how do you feel? Don't you feel completely listless? Isn't your energy sapped? It's almost as though you have given your soul away. Don't you feel as if you have been possessed by some force beyond your control? And then you think about what else you can say to correct what you've already said. You contemplate and reflect about how you can change those words, or you pray that person really didn't hear you anyway. Or you hope the person will forget what you said. You go to sleep thinking, "I hope he forgets it. I hope she forgets it. Well, maybe that person has a very good heart so she won't take advantage of what I said."

You are contemplating *after* you have said something, rather than *before* you say it — so you have double the amount of work. When you talk endlessly, when you say whatever you want to say, there is a kind of satisfaction for a while, but at the same time you are very confused about this satisfaction. And the confusion lasts for quite a while.

Having indulged in this sort of thing once, twice, or three times, then you begin to believe it is necessary. You think it's your style of speaking, and that's the way you will always speak. You think it's your way of exercising freedom of speech. This is when you say, "Well, I have the right. I'm an independent person. I'm a free individual. I can say whatever I want to say." And so you continue to make it part of your life. You use freedom of speech to serve your uncontrolled impulse to talk. You wind yourself up to a so-called "enthusiastic" level, as if that is what keeps your adrenal glands going, and you talk and talk and talk indiscriminately, without rhyme or reason.

Inevitably, this kind of behavior brings about a dwindling sense of self-worth and self-esteem, even if you are not aware of it at the moment. You make yourself less in your own eyes. And sooner or later, others, too, laugh at you. They consider you a reckless speaker who can't help herself. They learn to avoid you. "Here she comes," they say, glancing at their watches. "I have a meeting." In this state you have created for yourself, it becomes very difficult to sing God's glory. When there is no restraint in your speech, you diminish the power of your virtues.

Self-restraint is not opposed to freedom of speech. Truly speaking, it strengthens that great power. Restraint beautifies your speech. It makes your words even more worthwhile. As the verse in Proverbs says, "He who restrains his lips is prudent." Restraint honors the person who has the freedom to choose words and who has won control over his or her own speech. The word *prudent* has so many brilliant facets and degrees of meaning. It means "sagacious, cautious, discreet, judicious, sensible, careful, thrifty, astute, insightful, discerning, discriminating, intelligent, wise." With these qualities you are able to utilize the power of speech, the freedom of speech.

You cannot jeopardize these excellent characteristics in the name of freedom of speech. You must understand what freedom of speech truly stands for. When these virtues govern your choice of words, and when your words are spoken in the appropriate place, at the appropriate time, to the appropriate people, then freedom of speech reaches its zenith. It acquires its true glory. In this way you glorify freedom of speech. You must not use it as your servant. In fact, you should be able to glorify freedom of speech as the goddess Saraswati. This power is able to create a world that can transform and uplift the consciousness of others. It can give the people you come in contact with a great boost and assuage every heart weighed down with sorrow. With pure freedom of speech, you are truly able to comfort those who are sad. And such speech will also renew your own life continually. Just as love and respect must be renewed with each dawn, in the same way, speech must be contemplated before it is given birth in the form of syllables and words. Such is the divine power of speech that has shed its excesses and is free to soar. It is so much lighter; it experiences its own greatness. To experience this power of speech is truly being filled with enthusiasm and singing God's glory.

The poet-saint Sundardas often celebrates the power of speech and the principle of restraint in his songs. In one of them, he says:

> When a crow caws,
> when a donkey brays, or when an owl hoots,
> few people like to listen to them.
> But when a cuckoo or a nightingale sings,
> people stop and listen to their song.
> A person should speak with discrimination
> and not waste his *prāna* by chattering unnecessarily.
> Sundardas says, Either speak wisely or remain silent.[2]

On the spiritual path, *prāna*, the life-giving breath, is truly precious. The wise yogi watches over it carefully and keeps it safe from any wasteful tendency. *Prāna* is utterly essential in your spiritual practices. It is just as necessary for clear thinking and for living your life dharmically in this world. So Sundardas says, don't chatter unnecessarily and waste your *prāna*.

In Gurudev Siddha Peeth, Baba Muktananda used to maintain the discipline very strictly. He was very much opposed to people talking too much. When we were young, it seemed that he would appear any time we were engaged in unnecessary talking. We would feel, "The only time we are speaking a bit too much, he shows up. Why does it have to be like this?" We went on thinking like this for a long time. Continuous talking and continuous thinking without discipline truly do lead to delusion. And delusion doesn't stop right away, even when the fire of the Guru's presence blazes in front of you. Delusion is quite thick.

Finally, one day we discovered that if we didn't spend so much time talking, then Baba wouldn't catch us red-handed. It was because we had the tendency to talk unnecessarily that out of his compassion, he would show up once in a blue moon and let us know that we were wasting our *prāna*. So we began to observe silence whenever possible. And every time we were able to observe silence, we experienced the beauty of words, the beauty of speech. We were able to focus on Baba's words, we were able to listen to what others said with great care. In fact, we cherished what they said. And our inner experiences also deepened; we felt at one with our own Self. Then when we spoke, we were able to speak the Truth; we were able to share our love for one another rather than waste our time in talking about things that didn't make any sense to anyone — and weren't very fruitful either. We were able to save our *prāna*, our inbreath, our outbreath, the vital force. What we noticed was — and this was astonishing — that we had much more energy to work. We had more energy to offer selfless service in the ashram. We could give ourselves completely to working in the garden, to washing dishes, to washing clothes, to cleaning the Bhagawan Nityananda Temple. And we also had much more energy to perform other spiritual practices such as chanting and meditation. It was amazing to discover the power of silence — and that discovery gave us the freedom of speech.

When you speak without contemplation, whom does it serve? No one really. When you use words as weapons, what are you doing? You are far from singing God's glory. When your words are filled with disdain and you spread them around, then the destruction they cause is worse than a nuclear bomb — the fallout lasts through eternity. Useless speech diminishes the power of *prāna*, and then it no longer flows into your words. They become empty. Your words need the support of *prāna*, the breath of life, the vital force. When there is no *prāna* in your words, when there is no life force in what you say, your speech benefits no one. It has no life in it. It is dead.

There is a kind of speech that is of infinite benefit, that uplifts all who speak it and all who hear it. This is the enlivened mantra. By repeating the mantra, which is full of *prāna*, you energize and strengthen yourself. The mantra burns away the impurities in your speech and makes it luminous. It injects the nectarean rays of the Truth into every syllable. It inspires immortal words, words that come straight from the heart. Therefore, chanting the mantra is said to be the highest freedom, the culmination of the faculty of speech. The mantra makes you soar. It generates a greater and greater sense of affinity among people. It unites the hearts of all. When you chant the mantra, you are truly putting the freedom of speech to very good use. You are being filled with enthusiasm and singing God's glory.

Sundardas says, "Either speak wisely or remain silent." When silence is used discriminately, it is as powerful as dharmic speech. When speech is used judiciously, it is as strong as silence. Sometimes when people speak, you feel you are in the womb of great silence. Their words carry you to this realm of silence. You feel so much at peace with yourself. In fact, you seek their company. Their words are so nectarean that you want to be in their company when they speak.

Whenever Baba Muktananda described his Guru, he spoke about the quality of his silence, and the astounding impact of his words. In his book *Secret of the Siddhas*, Baba says:

> My Gurudev spoke very seldom — sometimes every few hours, sometimes once a day, or once every several days. Occasionally he would speak only once every three months or every six months. Then again he might not speak for nine months at a time. However, when Nityananda spoke

> even for ten minutes, it was more than enough for my entire life. I can now pass on his words to the whole world. A handful of the words of a Siddha contain great power and blaze with *shakti.*

You can always tell a person's good or bad character by the way he employs language. The power of words is such that it can cleave the darkest clouds and reveal the magnificence of the golden sun. Speech can instill sweet hope in the hearts of mankind. Or it can create such a sense of impending doom that all hope and courage drain away. When this is the case, you begin to see how delicate freedom of speech really is. The goddess Saraswati is so delicate. She is beautiful, she is strong, she is wonderful, she is benevolent. At the same time, like a flower, she is very delicate.

Recently, as I was walking through the lobby, I stopped to say goodbye to a family — the father, mother, and two wonderful, beautiful daughters. They were about to go home. The elder daughter, who is seven years old, looked very sad. She was leaning on her father's legs. So I said to her playfully, "You look so happy!"

She looked back at me with great big eyes. She still had a long face, yet she said very sweetly and softly, "I *was* happy when we were getting ready to come here."

She got her point across so clearly, so vividly, and so sensitively without negating what was said to her or hurting anyone's feelings. In her delicate and kind reply, she communicated so many of her feelings to me in such a positive manner. She could have easily said, "I am not happy! I don't want to go!" Instead, she chose to communicate her feelings without making me look wrong. That little girl truly showed freedom of speech.

God's very nature is freedom. Therefore, to experience freedom is to experience God. And to let your words flow freely from the deepest level of your being is to sing God's glory. Jnaneshwar Maharaj composed a beautiful description of one who uses freedom of speech in the most elevated way. Jnaneshwar says:

> His behavior is like the fruit of kindness, and his speech is full of compassion. . . .
>
> Even before he begins to speak, love springs from him, and compassion expresses itself before he says a word. . . .
>
> He avoids speaking unnecessarily, so that no one will be distressed or caused to suffer doubts,
>
> So that his words may not distract anyone from his work or cause anyone to fear or scorn him.
>
> He maintains silence so that he won't hurt others' feelings or cause them to frown. This is his attitude.
>
> If he is ever requested to speak, he speaks with affection, and those who listen feel he is their parent.
>
> His words sound like the resonant voice of God or the waters of the Ganges. They are as chaste as a virtuous wife who has grown old.
>
> His words are tender and true, moderate and sincere, like waves of nectar.
>
> His speech is free from sarcasm, hurting no one, never provoking ridicule or wounding deeply.
>
> In his speech there is no agitation or haste, no guile or false hope, doubt or deceit. He avoids such faults.
>
> O Arjuna, his look is steady and his brow unwrinkled.[3]

If you can use freedom of speech in this way, then you have truly honored freedom. By honoring freedom of speech, you honor every kind of freedom to which you are entitled. And you can enjoy the experience of freedom. You can speak and not have to bite your tongue. You can use the tongue, instead, to taste the good food this earth provides to nourish your being and your life, and you can speak true words from the deepest level of your being.

An Indian poet-saint named Bholenath describes how the perception of God in this world allows you to be filled with enthusiasm and gives you the freedom to sing God's glory:

> This entire universe is the garden of Shiva, the great Lord.
> It is meant for you to roam in.
> This universe is a mansion containing the mirror
> of Lord Shiva.
> Whoever looks in it with the feeling of being one
> with the great Lord
> sees his own divine image everywhere,
> sees the great Lord everywhere.[4]

Allow your entire being to be filled with enthusiasm. Be thankful that you can truly sing God's glory as you recognize God in each moment, as you offer kindness to others, as you are able to sit in silence and experience the power of silence within. Contemplate the power of silence and the freedom of speech.

To let your words flow freely from the deepest level of your being is to be filled with enthusiasm and sing God's glory.

With great respect, with great love, I welcome you all with all my heart.

*Sadgurunāth mahārāj kī jay!*

*Chapter 6*

# Discarding the Burden of Self-Hatred

With great respect, with great love, I welcome you all with all my heart.

Living in the divine experience of enthusiasm, staying in touch with the divinity that abides within you, letting it sing through all your actions, allowing this great glory to shine forth and lend its radiance to your whole day: this is our theme and this is our goal.

To wake up in the morning and feel refreshed, to apply yourself to your duties and feel contented, to accept all that is beautiful and feel wonderful, to let go of all that binds you and still feel superb, to recognize the Consciousness shimmering in everything around you, to be anchored in this awareness, and to truly experience your own inner divinity, your own greatness: this is our philosophy. Be jubilant, be full of zest, be filled with enthusiasm and sing God's glory.

An Indian poet-saint named Ravidas sings God's glory by describing his intimate relationship with the indwelling Lord:

> O Lord, You are the sandalwood and I am the water:
> Your fragrance permeates my entire being.
> Your fragrance pervades everything.
>
> O Lord, You are the cloud and I am the *chātaka* bird;
> in the forest of my mind I gaze at You,
> as the *chakora* bird gazes at the moon.
> O Lord, You are the sandalwood and I am the water.[1]

Every person is filled with greatness and surrounded by greatness. There is so much love within and without. Therefore, everyone has the right to be enthusiastic; everyone has reason to be filled with wonder. This entire universe is filled with wonder, God's wonder. Yet all too often, people find themselves unable to experience enthusiasm or to sing God's glory. This very simple and rewarding awareness becomes difficult to put into practice and difficult to maintain. Yet what could be more natural than this awareness? Even the tiniest glimpse of God's all-encompassing love fills the heart with gratitude. What darkness could shut out so much light? What can it be made of?

One of the thickest shadows that falls over the heart is hatred. In the *Bhagavad Gītā*, Lord Krishna tells Arjuna many times that only he who is free from hatred experiences serenity. In Patanjali's *Yoga Sūtras*, hatred, *dvesha*, is mentioned as one of the afflictions of the mind. Such preoccupation prevents a seeker from experiencing his own inner Self. Hatred is utterly contrary to one's true nature. So it is very strange that it arises with such force in a human being, and yet most people feel it at one time or another. It seems that when a person believes he is unable to ascend higher, he begins to wallow in hatred. Somehow hatred seems easier to arrive at than the goal he wants to reach but thinks he cannot. And once hatred comes over a person, it is so corrosive; it affects everything it touches. It taints everything one thinks about. The *Mahābhārata*, the great Indian epic about dharma, says this about hatred: If you hate someone, you do not consider him to be a good person, even if he is learned and wise. If someone is dear to you, his actions look so noble. If you hate someone, all his actions are filled with faults.

Hatred enters the system like a deadly venom. Once you drink it, you fall under its influence. It completely separates you from the fountain of enthusiasm, your innate inspiration. You are thirsty, yet you cannot drink. Hatred dries you up and consumes you from inside. Worst of all, it blinds you to the goodness in all things. *Hatred* is a very strong word — practically a curse.

Yet there are people who find a strange enjoyment in firing up their adrenals with hate. They hold on to hatred as if their whole life depended on it. It is their stimulant, their addiction.

Of course, most true seekers would shrink from injecting hatred into their feelings for others. Yet these very people have no qualms about applying hatred to themselves. That is where hatred usually begins — with yourself. How can you even think about having enthusiasm and singing God's glory when you are constantly under the attack of the ego, the adversary of goodness? How can you feel enthusiasm when you are constantly under the attack of self-hatred?

Self-hatred is a devastating frame of mind. It is like a virulent disease. What happens when self-hatred invades your mind and oppresses your awareness? Everywhere you turn, it stands before you. Everywhere you bow, you experience self-hatred.

How does a mind riddled with self-hatred respond? When you condemn your very existence, when you detest yourself as a human being, when you criticize every word that comes out of your own mouth, when you put down every effort you make, when you speak to yourself as someone who is always falling short, always accomplishing less than other people, never coming through — what effect do you think this has on your own mind? What must your mind think of itself? What is the state of your consciousness?

And what about the heart? It is a witness, constantly watching everything that takes place within yourself. What must happen to your heart? How likely is it that your innate enthusiasm will be revealed when your inner environment is filled with self-hatred? How can you be free to experience the deepest relationship with God? How can you give yourself to serving God? How can you sing God's glory as Saint Ravidas did? How can you be free like him to experience the close connection, the deepest relationship with God? Ravidas says:

O Lord, You are the sandalwood and I am the water:
Your fragrance permeates my entire being.
Your fragrance pervades everything.

O Lord, You are the lamp and I am the wick:
Your light shines forth day in and day out.

What happens when self-hatred comes in contact with your good qualities, your divine virtues? Doesn't it swallow up every nourishing feeling, each delicious thought, every sweet vibration, each healing impulse? Unfortunately, self-hatred is not transformed by its contact with good qualities. It remains what it is. It is very strong. Its darkness consumes all the greatness that shines before it.

As a modern writer says, "An hour spent in hatred is an eternity withdrawn from love."

Truly, self-hatred is a pitiful state of mind. It would evoke such sympathy if only it weren't so self-involved, so self-absorbed, so oblivious to others. Self-hatred is a sure sign of egocentricity. It is a way of saying, "Look at me. Come and support me. Give me attention. Hey, look, it's me!" And, like all the activities of the ego, self-hatred plunges you deeper and deeper into a world of self-defeat.

You might ask, "How and why does self-hatred gain such a foothold in a person's life?" There isn't any one single reason. However, lack of spiritual understanding definitely plays a big part. When you refuse to recognize the great Principle, the presence of God, within yourself and within everyone else, then you leave yourself open to all the disorders of the ego.

Beyond the ego lies the perfect I-consciousness, the supreme Self, *pūrno'ham vimarsha*, the great Light, the great Knowledge. This perfect I-consciousness is the substratum of all that is and is not. It is the divine power behind all your thoughts and feelings and actions. This is who you truly are — *pūrno'ham vimarsha*, the perfect I-consciousness, the awareness "I am That, I am Shiva."

The amazing thing is that not only do people deny their own true nature, they also identify with every negativity that arises in the mind. "Ah, yes! I'm so bad. I'm so miserable. I've always known I'm a sinner." They feel such an intimate bond with their self-created negativities. They preserve them so carefully. "I am so bad. As soon as you get to know me, you won't like me. Just you wait and see." Self-hatred.

Once a celestial being who was visiting the Earth came to a vast forest. There he found a creature with a thousand arms and a thousand legs, and each of these limbs was moving constantly. He couldn't sit still for a single moment. In one of his hands he carried a club covered with spikes, and he would beat himself with it over and over again. With each blow he would cry out in pain and panic, saying, "Please don't hit me. Don't hit me again. Please don't!" Trying to avoid the blows he was suffering from his own hand, he would run first in one direction and then in another. He was so frightened that he didn't pay attention to where he was going, and he fell into a deep well.

It took him a long time to climb out of this well, and when he did, he sat on the edge, panting and exhausted. But as soon as he caught his breath, he was up again and beating himself with his hideous weapon. Then he ran into a dense thicket. When he came out a few moments later, he was scratched and bleeding and covered with thorns. Next he fled into a beautiful grove of banana trees. There were songbirds and wildflowers and fresh, luscious, colorful tropical fruit, but he didn't notice any of it. He was blinded by fear and loathing, and he sat shaking and screaming and beating himself up.

Finally, out of compassion, the celestial being restrained him. "Be calm," he said. "Relax. Just breathe. Be calm. Why are you hurting yourself like this? Who are you running away from? Where are you going?"

But the creature couldn't listen to the beautiful celestial

being who was speaking to him so gently. He couldn't see the benevolent smile, or feel the touch that was softer than velvet. He couldn't sense the compassion that was streaming toward him. In fact, he thought this visitor was his enemy. "Get away!" he screamed out. "Don't touch me! Don't talk to me!" The prospect of leaving that dark forest of cruelty in which he lived all his life was unthinkable to him.

A sage who was meditating in a cave nearby came out of meditation and opened his eyes. He spoke to the celestial being and said, "Listen. This is the Earth planet. This is *samsāra*, the world of birth and death. This creature that you've tried to console is nothing but the mind. The mind with its countless creations. The mind that creates everything endlessly and forever punishes itself with its own tendencies. Those thousand arms and legs are nothing but the tendencies of the mind."

The celestial being nodded his head gently and disappeared.

Have you ever found yourself almost boasting about self-hatred, trying to impress yourself and others with a long litany of your defects? You say, "I am plagued by negative emotions, and therefore, I don't like myself." Have you ever done that?

"I have committed so many sins, and therefore, I don't like myself."

"I have such a poor character, and therefore, I don't like myself."

"My performance at work is mediocre, and therefore, I don't like myself."

"Other people look down on me, and therefore, I don't like myself either."

"I am not able to love anyone the way I think I should, and therefore, I don't like myself."

"I am haunted by painful memories, and therefore, I don't like myself."

"I am visited by afflictions, and therefore, I don't like myself."

"I always get the worst end of the deal — always — and therefore, I don't like myself."

"People around me are usually so happy. Look at them, so happy, sickeningly happy, and I am not, and therefore, I don't like myself."

"I am tormented by a lack of self-worth, and I hate myself."

"I am never good enough at anything, and so I hate myself."

"I am the butt of jokes, and therefore, I hate myself."

"My behavior is never pleasing to anyone, and therefore, I just don't like myself."

You might be thinking, "Stop! That's enough! I get the point!"

But let's stay with it for a few more minutes. Let's see why else you might hate yourself. After all, you've been hoarding these thoughts for centuries. Why not take them out and look at them? What are some of the other ways you express self-hatred?

You can't seem to chant properly, and therefore, you hate yourself. Your seva is not appreciated, and therefore, you hate yourself. Meditation doesn't come easily for you, and therefore, you hate yourself. You don't have a generous heart, and therefore, you don't like yourself. You are not well educated, and therefore, you hate yourself. You can't love the Guru as deeply as others seem to, and therefore, you hate yourself. You are not able to be as charitable as you think you should be, and therefore, you hate yourself. You are not religious, and therefore, you hate yourself. The reasons for self-hatred go on and on.

To one degree or another, self-hatred feeds on thoughts and feelings like these — always comparing yourself with others, always creating goals for yourself that you can't fulfill. Of course, we're not talking about stretching your limits and seeing if you can reach a distant but possible goal. That is different. Here you are setting yourself up for guaranteed failure. However, when you really use your discrimination and scrutinize each of your so-called faults and shortcomings, you find that they don't hold up under investigation. In fact, they have no strength at all.

If you insist on coming from that space of lack, then you are pretending to be like a dung beetle that can only survive on dung. You are behaving like a crow that insists on a strict diet of garbage. You are like a buffalo that is only happy when it wallows in mud. In India, sometimes you come across beautiful lakes and ponds where you find buffaloes blissfully dredging up the mud and wallowing in it. The mud feels like velvet to them. You are acting like a buffalo. You are emulating someone who builds a castle of garbage and then chooses to live in it. That is self-hatred.

There was once a flower seller who was great friends with a fisherman. They were truly great friends. One day the flower seller invited the fisherman to come to dinner and to spend the night at his home. The fisherman gladly accepted his friend's invitation. When the day came, the florist welcomed his guest with open arms. He had decorated his home with hundreds of fragrant flowers. And he had taken special care with the room where the fisherman was going to sleep. It was full of sweet-smelling blossoms, truly fit for a king.

After a good meal, the two friends retired to their respective rooms for a good night's sleep. The florist was soon snoring happily. He was so pleased that he had been able to play host to his old friend and cook for him and offer him so many fragrant flowers.

The fisherman, however, could not sleep a wink. He tossed and turned and pulled the covers over his head. He even pretended to snore, thinking the sound might put him to sleep. He opened the windows for fresh air, but still he had a splitting headache.

When morning came, the florist gently knocked on the fisherman's door.

"Yes, come in," said the fisherman. "Please come in."

The florist opened the door and was shocked at what he

saw. The fisherman was sitting on the bed looking quite dejected. His hair was disheveled and he had many new lines in his face. The florist was crestfallen. He couldn't understand what had happened. How could he have been so insensitive to his guest?

"What's the matter? Are you all right? Didn't you sleep? Why didn't you call me? You are my guest and I would have come running. Please tell me what's happening. I feel so bad."

"Let's get out of this room. I can't stand it. Please get me out of here," begged the fisherman.

"Yes, of course," said the florist, and he helped the fisherman out of the room. "Now, what's happening? Can you tell me?"

The fisherman said, "Listen, all those flowers — they're just too fragrant. They've blocked up my sinuses. I can't breathe. I couldn't breathe all night, but I didn't want to be rude. I didn't want to disturb you. I didn't want to just walk out, but please let me go back. I want to go back to the fish market where a man can breathe."

The florist understood. "Of course. But first, let me get the cloth that covers your fish basket. You left it outside last night." He ran to the empty fish basket and picked up the cloth that covered it. Then he returned and held the cloth close to his friend's face.

"Oh, thank you," said the fisherman, breathing a big sigh of relief. "Thank you for reviving me. Thank you, thank you, thank you."

And then, very happily, the fisherman went back to the fish market. And the florist, with great understanding, went to the flower market.

Listen carefully. Self-hatred is not your only choice. When you look deep within, when you experience the Self within the heart, you realize how much you have underestimated yourself. Truly, you have all the power you need to make any change in your life. You are capable of achieving your highest aspirations. You are truly great. Stop undermining your own greatness and your own divinity. You are great. This is what all the sages say.

If you want to experience the true greatness of your inner being, you must break the chain of self-hatred, link by link. You can begin anywhere. You don't have to wait to go to the Bhagawan Nityananda Temple before you break the chain of self-hatred. You don't have to wait until the Intensive comes to break the chain of self-hatred. You don't have to take a bath and purify yourself first, and then think about breaking the chain of self-hatred. No! At any point you can do it — link by link. Stop trampling on the goodness of your heart. Stop beating yourself up with negative beliefs.

On the spiritual path, self-hatred is especially harmful. According to the Ba'al Shem Tov, a great mystic of the Jewish tradition, the sincere seeker must learn not to brood on his faults. Quite the opposite. As a modern scholar writes, the Ba'al Shem Tov deeply believed that

> . . . a man torn by inner struggles was not yet ready to come to God. Hence his comments denouncing excessive worry about minor sins. Brooding on one's sinfulness, he taught, was merely a trick by the [forces of evil] to keep man far from God. The service of God requires the deepest joy, and such joy cannot be experienced in a divided self. Repent of evil, know that God in His love accepts your penitence, and return to serve Him with joy and wholeness.[2]

All the great beings say, serve God with joy and wholeness, with your entire being, with *pūrno'ham vimarsha*, the awareness "I am perfect, I am the great Light, the great Knowledge." If your inner battles do not come from noble aspirations, then no matter how ferociously you struggle, they will take you nowhere. If you must struggle, then wrestle with your self-hatred so that you release its hold on you. If you must struggle, then endeavor to approach the divine Presence. If you must struggle, then strive to serve the Lord. If you must struggle, then yearn to attain God's love. If you must struggle, then use that energy to embrace God's creation. If you must struggle, then turn your effort to releasing the enthusiasm within yourself, to serving God with joy and wholeness. If you must struggle, let your burning aspiration be to have the experience that Saint Ravidas describes:

> O Lord, You are the sandalwood and I am the water:
> Your fragrance permeates my entire being.
> Your fragrance pervades everything.
>
> O Lord, You are the pearl and I am the thread.
> Being with You, I feel as if gold has acquired sweet fragrance.

No scripture on earth has ever preached a gospel of self-hatred or resentment. Resentment only takes you deeper into its own darkness. Then what will rescue you from your own self-hatred? The antidote to the poison of self-hatred is contentment, *santosha.* Contentment returns your heart to its golden state. Contentment anoints your heart with the healing balm of serenity. Contentment makes the fire of God blaze very high, from a place deep within you. Contentment renews your spirit so that your whole being sings God's glory.

Baba Muktananda said: "If you worship God within, the results of that worship will appear right inside you in the form of contentment and fulfillment. There is a source of great contentment hidden within you. It is supremely blissful, and its name is love."

Loving God and serving Him with joy and enthusiasm, joy

and wholeness, joy and singing His glory — that is what brings you into the light of God, the light of your own divinity. Therefore, be filled with enthusiasm and sing God's glory. Whatever you are, you are precious to God. Won't you please take this to heart? Whatever you are, you are precious to God. You can always say to yourself, "I am very precious to God. I am loved by God." Just think of all the things God does for you. Then you will be able to believe that He loves you.

Sometimes, when people narrowly avert an automobile accident or are suddenly spared an oncoming misfortune, they see with their own eyes that God is saving them. Automatically, they feel gratitude and recognize God's love. A simple incident like that makes you realize how many times God must have saved you when you were not aware that anything had happened. This is true not only of ordinary accidents, but of so-called spiritual accidents as well. So many times you are tortured by doubts — doubts about your spiritual path, doubts about your spiritual practices, doubts about your ability to progress on the path, doubts about your own Guru, about the teachings, doubts about the divinity within you. And then God comes and rescues you in one way or another. This is why the Indian sages and saints always pray to God, to the Master, to the Guru: "Please, no matter what my mind thinks, no matter what I feel, save me, keep me on the path." In fact, the saints pray continuously: "O God, I understand my mind is fickle, my mind wanders everywhere. Please don't look at my faults. Give me the strength to stay on the path and to love You, to stay devoted to You." Whatever you think you are, know that you are precious to God. God is always protecting you. Be filled with enthusiasm and sing God's glory.

You can tell someone sweetly how good they are, or you can sing their glory aloud, "How good you are!" You can whisper it, or you can sing it at the top of your lungs. You can quietly go and put a flower in someone's room, or you can send a singing message that says, "These flowers are meant to show how much I love you." You can nod your head in agreement with someone, or you can let them know sweetly that you don't agree with them but you still like them. All this is singing God's glory. You sing God's glory when you acknowledge other people's glory and recognize God's presence within them.

Baba Muktananda was a great enemy of belittling yourself. He urged all seekers to hold the highest awareness of themselves. He taught everyone that spiritual progress consists of expanding your capacity to perceive God's light in everything. Baba's words were always filled with enthusiasm, and they helped countless seekers to recognize their own worth. In fact, just by coming into his presence, people experienced their own worthiness. If there was one thing that Baba staunchly asserted time and time again, it was the innate worthiness of each human being. In so many ways he said, "Know your own worthiness. Respect it."

To Baba, impurities were nothing compared to the light of God. His own being always roared with divinity, and so in his presence, your impurities would be blasted away. Vibrations of love for God poured out of Baba like a rushing river, and so in his presence, you too would experience very strong, deep devotion for God. Burdens like self-hatred couldn't last around Baba. They exposed themselves as fragments of ignorance, shards of a past that you were leaving behind. Baba wrote and spoke about the process of purification in many different ways. Once he said:

> You should not belittle yourself by seeing only your faults. In fact, you should keep congratulating yourself on your exceptional good fortune. You should keep thinking, "I have become completely pure." You should not recall your past sinful deeds; you should only remember the Lord, who lives within you.

> You should disengage your mind from feelings of guilt; this is just a phase of the mind. Instead, you should sing the divine Name as much as you can. It takes only one second, one moment, for you to become pure, particularly if you are in a sacred place — in a temple, or the Guru's abode. You should not identify yourself with the innumerable fancies or thoughts that arise in your mind from moment to moment. Instead, you should identify yourself with the source from which all these fancies arise. That source is the Self, and the Self is you.

Keep yourself aware of your supreme inner purity. The divine light within you cannot be affected or bound by any fancy that may arise in your mind. When you become aware of your own supreme Reality, you also perceive the bond of love that unites you with God. You are filled with contentment, you are totally free. That is why you walk the spiritual path. Singing of this experience, the poet-saint Ravidas says:

> O Lord, You are the sandalwood and I am the water:
> Your fragrance permeates my entire being.
> Your fragrance pervades everything.
>
> O Lord, You are the Master and I am Your servant.
> Please allow Ravidas to experience such devotion constantly.

O Lord, says Ravidas, allow me to experience great love for You. Allow me to have such devotion for You. It is better to serve the Highest than to serve self-hatred. It is better to serve the supreme Being who is pure love than to be the servant of poisonous, negative feelings about yourself. Baba used to say, no matter how you are feeling, just chant. No matter what you are going through, make time for meditation. No matter what circumstances you are experiencing in your life, perform seva, selfless service. Even if you are filled with sorrow, offer a smile to others. Others' sorrows are much deeper than yours. Be happy.

Always think of doing something wonderful, no matter what your state of mind. Don't wait for your mind to become happy to do something good. Go ahead and do something good now. Then your goodness will shine forth, and you will experience how much you want to sing God's glory and perceive divinity within everyone.

With great respect, with great love, I welcome you all with all my heart.

*Sadgurunāth mahārāj kī jay!*

*Chapter 7*

# The Jewel of Constancy

With great respect, with great love, I welcome you all with all my heart.

Be filled with enthusiasm and sing God's glory — this seems like a very simple message, a straightforward theme. And yet, the more you look into it, the more subtlety and depth you discover. What does it take to fill yourself with God? What are the virtues, the foundation stones, of boundless enthusiasm? How do you keep yourself open to the experience of God's glory? How can you constantly remain in the abode of enthusiasm? And what will continually inspire you to celebrate God's glory?

Many of you have made resolutions to let God's energy pour through you. You have resolved to make space in your heart for God to abide. You have resolved to walk through the days and nights seeing God's presence everywhere, allowing His energy to work through you. One of the greatest things I have noticed about resolutions is that once you have made them, God hears them. And then, even if you forget them, somehow, out of His compassion, He fulfills your resolutions anyway.

Ever since people have begun to contemplate this message, the most wondrous enthusiasm has been coursing through their days and nights, sparkling like clusters of stars, dancing like the light on flowing water. Many people have shared that their nightmares are gone, and their dreams are filled with joy, contentment, and beautiful visions. To let God's energy pour through you, you must recognize His presence all around you. You must learn to find Him in every word, every thought, every object, every situation, every emotion, and every unit of time.

In India, it is traditional to sing God's glory when you first wake up in the morning. You remember the supreme Consciousness within. You call to mind the attributes of the Almighty. Just by remembering them, just by giving voice to them, you bring them into your day. You are able to carry the love of God, the love of the Guru, the love of the supreme Self, into all your actions. One of these morning prayers is by a sage of the Vedantic tradition. He says:

> Every morning I meditate on the *ātman*,
> the supreme Consciousness that throbs in my heart.
> It is Existence, Consciousness, and Bliss Absolute.
> The supreme Self is the ultimate state of the *paramahamsas*,
> the great beings.
> To yogis, it is known as *turīya*,
> which is the eternal Knower of the other three states:
> waking, dream, and deep sleep.
> The inner Self is pure, indivisible Brahman,
> the supreme Absolute,
> and I am That.
> I am not this body composed of the five elements.[1]

"Every morning I meditate on the supreme Consciousness that throbs in my heart." Truly, how beautiful it is to awake each morning and remember this prayer, to let it resonate in your heart and in your being. It is a defining moment — to begin your daily activities by embracing the light of supreme Consciousness, by having the awareness "I am Shiva, I am the Truth," by affirming that you are That. When you begin your day full of light, full of bliss, full of awareness and understanding, supreme Consciousness lights the way, filling your entire day with bliss. It keeps you alert every moment and also brings about great serenity.

Just as the heart must pump blood continuously through your system, similarly, the wisdom of the sages must constantly be infused into your subtle system. The wisdom of the sages truly defines the purpose of human life. This divine wisdom sustains your enthusiasm and your yearning to sing God's glory.

Brahmananda, a poet-saint of India, was filled with enthusiasm. Having received the Guru's grace, he constantly praised God and prayed that he would always sing His glory. In one of his songs, he says:

> O Lord, may I always remember You in my heart.
> Be merciful and show me Your true form.[2]

A true devotee always prays to the Lord, to the Guru, to show His true form, His *satsvarūpa.*

Now listen carefully. No matter how good something may be; no matter how beneficial; no matter how wonderful, important, or advantageous; no matter how lovely or necessary; how profitable, vital, nurturing, or invaluable; no matter how useful, essential, or even indispensable something may be, human beings are apt to forget it. And what is the result? There are disturbances of all kinds and magnitudes. From the smallest and most insignificant oversight to an earthshaking blunder, forgetfulness always leaves a trail of consequences. Forgetfulness is so common, however, that people seem to accept it as part of the human condition. They forget people's names, forget to button their shirt before they leave home, forget where they put their glasses, forget a loved one's birthday or anniversary, forget to pick up a child from school, forget to pay their bills, forget to clean the bathroom even when it is their turn. They forget to water the plants, to fill out forms for the bank, to turn off the stove when they leave the house, to lock the door, to secure a tiny rivet in a space ship, to "save" on the computer — there goes all that work! They forget to exercise, to acknowledge the boss's newborn child, to pick up the vegetables at the grocery store. The list goes on and on. All these acts of forgetfulness can cause a painful rift in your relationships. And even though others may claim that you act this way because you don't love them, truly speaking, all that has taken place is forgetfulness. These instances of forgetfulness can make people lose faith and confidence in your abilities. In fact, you begin to get a name for yourself — you are called an unreliable person. Your forgetfulness earns you a title.

What is the one thing all these lapses have in common? What fault do they reveal? In all these instances one thing is missing: constancy. These examples all represent personal responsibilities. They are all things that require regular attention. When the continuity is broken, an element of disruption and messiness enters your life. Forgetfulness gives rise to agitation. It creates misunderstandings. It can sometimes even lead to genuine danger. And then, the efforts you have to make to undo the wrong, to stabilize the rocking boat, are always much more demanding than the thing you forgot to do in the first place.

But think about this. If forgetfulness in small matters creates such havoc, such disarray, and upsets so many people, imagine what happens when you forget the great Self, which abides within you, the supreme Consciousness throbbing in your heart. What kind of imbalance must that create — forgetting God's love, forgetting the Truth, forgetting the wisdom of the heart? Are these things to think about only once in a while? The wisdom of the sages? Divine virtues? The goodness in everyone? The living Consciousness in all beings? When there is no constancy in your awareness of the highest, what must the Heart of all hearts go through? What must your inner being endure when you forget supreme Consciousness?

Out of compassion, God constantly helps true seekers. In the front of Shree Muktananda Ashram stands a statue of Nataraj, an image of the great Lord Shiva's dance of grace. The statue portrays a beautiful statement about God's compassion. When you look carefully at Nataraj you can see that Shiva's lower foot is holding down a tiny demon. You can actually experience the weight of His foot. This demon is called *apasmara*, forgetfulness. He symbolizes the state of the limited ego that has forgotten its true nature. The ego always acts out of ignorance because it has forgotten the indwelling Self. Lord Shiva dances on the demon as an act of grace. He is putting an end to forgetfulness so that a seeker can remember his own true nature, so that he can recall, "I am Shiva, I am the Truth." Standing there by the sacred fire in front of the ashram, Nataraj reminds you to wake up, to emerge from the darkness of forgetfulness into the light of the Truth. It is a call to embrace the great Light.

Understand one thing: if you want to be filled with enthusiasm and sing God's glory, you must develop constancy. You must allow this message to be woven throughout your being. If you are constant in this, forgetfulness will not take root in your awareness. It will become thinner and thinner and eventually disappear.

Constancy is a very beautiful practice. By remembering to perceive God's shimmering beauty everywhere and in everything, you fill yourself with immeasurable grace, immeasurable peace and delight. When you say something to someone that is not so uplifting, think about it. See if you can say it a little differently. In this way, you recognize God in another person; you realize you are speaking to God. You can practice this with animals also. When you speak to an animal, understand you are speaking to God who dwells in this animal. Many people say that they speak to their trees and plants and flowers. This may sound strange to those who don't believe in such things, but the truth of the matter is whenever you speak lovingly to trees and plants and flowers, they grow in abundance and shed more of God's glory on your life. In fact, they sparkle. You can tangibly feel the presence of God in them, and the fragrance they emit is undeniably strong. Even in areas where people say plants won't grow, if you regularly speak to the plants very sweetly and lovingly, even just once a day, they will flourish. Just that much constancy makes the difference.

When your actions arise from this center of awareness, they can uplift humanity. If you want to uplift humanity, you cannot do it just by handing out clothes, or distributing money, or teaching about a higher standard of living. You cannot truly help people if you just create more and more programs for those who are sick and poor. You must come from that beautiful space within yourself, supreme Consciousness. And there must be constancy in your remembrance of this. That is when all your actions bear fruit.

If you want to cross a wide river, you must build a bridge all the way from one shore to the other. If it is built only halfway, your journey comes to an abrupt end. The same is true if you are building a house. You must follow through with every detail completely. Otherwise, if your effort is interrupted, if you forget to do one thing or another, the house will not be safe. Things will leak, they will fall apart. They will be neither safe nor comfortable.

Look around you. There is so much constancy in your life. So many wonderful people exist in your life — sweet people, considerate and giving people. Their constant presence in your life gives you happiness. Think of Nature. She is constantly mesmerizing us with her beauty and teaching us great lessons through her abundance. The movement of the stars in the heavens is constant, and it instructs us in the natural laws that govern creation. Look at your own body. Become aware of the constancy of your own breathing. The breath, the simple breath that comes in and goes out. Just imagine if this constancy were to waver. What would happen? The physical body would experience uneasiness and panic. If that constancy failed completely, life would come to an end. Truly, the same thing applies to everything in your life, whether it is spiritual or mundane. There is such constancy in this universe.

God's love is constant. Whatever you think of in your life that is constant and magnificent brings you back to the same thing: God's love. That is what is constant in your life — God's love and God's support. There is no break in God's support for you. Whether you turn to God or not, God is always watching over you. God never turns His face away from you. The Indian scriptures say God has a thousand faces, a thousand arms and legs. God has heads everywhere. If you are behind God, God is watching you. If you are before God, God is watching you. No matter where you turn, God is watching over you. God sees everything, everywhere.

The poet-saint Dadu Deena Dayal says:

> O Lord we may forget You,
>     but You never forget us.
> We may stray from the path,
>     but You never let us wander too far.
> When we forget You, You come to meet us.[3]

Haven't you experienced that? If you have ever tried to run away from the spiritual path, from your own goodness, you run and run until finally you collapse. Then right before you, right in your heart, you experience God's love. Or sometimes you cry about something; you cry and you sob all day long. You fall asleep crying, but when you wake up, you feel so good, so refreshed. What is that freshness? Where did that goodness come from? It is God's hand, God's love. So Dadu goes on to say:

> When we get separated, You rush to embrace us,
> You come looking for us.
> You have that feeling of oneness with us,
> even when we don't feel one with You.
> Dadu Deena Dayal says, O Lord, have compassion on me
> and reveal Yourself to me.
> Show me Your true form.

On the subject of constancy, Baba Muktananda once said: "If you were to study the life and character of the saints who achieved the highest realization, you would understand that it did not come to them in an instant. They had to work very hard for it. They had to pass through a prolonged phase of intense *tapasya* and discipline. You must never forget that."

There are several layers of meaning to the practice of constancy on the spiritual path. *Constancy* means remembrance, the awareness of the Self. It means consistency, the ongoing ability to translate your intention into practice. It also means continuity, unwavering fidelity to your highest aspirations. In short, *constancy* is a word that combines discipline and faith, which are the root of all attainments.

When you think of consistency, it reminds you of the abilities of some professors and scholars. If you give them one short word or term, they are able to write a whole commentary on it. They can translate just one single word into the most beautiful teaching and convey the very meaning you were feeling in your heart. These scholars can do this because they constantly study the scriptures. They continually try to imbibe wisdom; and therefore, they live the scriptures day in and day out — in their waking state and in their dream state also. For this reason, contemplation goes on all the time. They can take a leaf from a tree and speak about it so philosophically that you want to preserve that leaf for eternity. You want to put it on your *pūjā*. You want to look at it and receive its grace because they have made God come alive, they have made the Truth come alive in that leaf.

All the scriptures and all the great beings who have achieved something worthwhile emphasize constancy in spiritual life. When there is constancy, you are able to understand what others are saying because you have been using your mind for contemplation. You are able to listen so carefully that you can penetrate the words, whether spoken or written. You are able to enter into the heart of the word, to reach the center of the terminology, and you become inspired by that. This is how understanding should be.

Baba Muktananda said he didn't like people to repeat his words like parrots. He wanted people to become inspired by what he said and go deeper into the teachings and make them their own. He wanted people to see the light of their own hearts in these teachings and live from that space. Baba said, don't imitate the Guru — follow the Guru's teachings. What does this mean? It means walking deeper into the teachings and seeing the light with your own eyes.

Although a prolonged phase of discipline may look and sound like a monotonous way to live, it really isn't. Constancy is very exciting. When you truly practice constancy, when you embrace continuity and let your practice be *nirantara*, a constant unbroken flow, an incredible amount of enthusiasm is released. And it keeps increasing. Constancy has great power.

When all your activities have a deeper meaning and a greater purpose, then you take immense comfort and support from being punctual, from being consistent and reliable. You see your activities as an extension of your own being. Rather than thinking anxiously that you must get something done, you think about giving your energy to it. You give it your attention, your vibrations, your loving care.

So many people yearn for excellence. They want to do everything excellently. And they want to receive excellent praise as well. But sometimes they flinch at the amount of continuous, excellent effort it takes to produce excellent results. It is by doing something constantly, faithfully, and with steadfastness that you are able to achieve something worth praising. Haven't you noticed that when someone has been doing something constantly, you automatically respect them? If someone has been married, say, for forty years, you respect them for maintaining that constant relationship. If someone has been at a job for twenty years, you respect them for their loyalty. The same is true on the spiritual path. If someone has been on the same path year after year, you have tremendous respect for them because you know they have been through ups and downs, hard times and good times, dark times and times filled with light. You know what it takes to stay with something over a long time, and respect naturally grows in your heart. Seeing goodness in others is singing God's glory. Constancy is truly beautiful. It doesn't have to be boring; it can be exhilarating.

The English word *constant* is derived from the Latin word *constare*, which means "to stand firm." Whenever you stand firmly behind your principles, promises, goals, aspirations, resolutions, creations, and offerings, then you are able to experience their fruits. You are nurtured by the stance you have taken. You are supported by the process it sets in motion. Truly speaking, everyone appreciates regularity — particularly in others. Even if you think regularity is not your style, you do appreciate it in other people. By the same token, everyone abhors inconsistency in others. Even if people think they are personally excused from the obligation to be consistent, they do not give the same license to anyone else. It is a general rule of human behavior that people expect supreme constancy from the world around them.

When you are married, each spouse expects constancy in the other. When you are in a teacher-student relationship, both the teacher and the student expect constancy. If there is a disruption or an interference with this constancy, both parties become exasperated. They become provoked, incensed, and irritated beyond belief: "You come on time every day! Otherwise you'll make me angry!" And that's only the beginning. They have many other reactions as well — both reasonable and unreasonable — and they are quite ready to verbalize their feedback.

Human beings, by nature, are creatures who like constancy. What do you feel when your plane is late? Or when you have been sitting in a restaurant for hours and your food hasn't arrived? How do you feel when a teacher doesn't show up for your lesson without warning? Or when you fall ill and your doctor has taken an unscheduled vacation? How do you feel when your car won't start? When the bus doesn't arrive on time? When other people come very late to a chanting and meditation program? What is your state of mind when you meditate in the Intensive and a vision doesn't appear quickly? How do you feel when you are the only one who shows up to wash the dishes?

Constancy is an inherent part of your nature. It is hard enough when the outside world frustrates your desire for order, punctuality, and regularity. But when you go against your own true nature, what happens? The result is restlessness, turbulence, and an insidious sense of unease. In the scriptures you often come across the word *constant* — in Sanskrit *sadā, sarvadā.* In the *Vishnu Sahasranāma,* it is said:

> Vishnu, the great Lord, has neither beginning nor end. He is the great Lord of all the worlds, the witness of the world. By constantly praising Him, one can pass beyond all sorrows.[4]

The *Devī Gītā* associates constancy with vigilance. In one of its verses, the Goddess says:

> The yogi who meditates on Me with constant vigilance and is impelled by supreme devotion knows that he is not separate from Me.[5]

The *Shrīmad Bhāgavatam* links constancy to service and study of the scriptures. It says:

> Constant service to holy men and constant study of the highest scriptures remove whatever negative tendencies obstruct the dawning of devotion. Then, firm and unswerving devotion to God arises.[6]

The *Kulārnava Tantra* associates constancy with mantra repetition. It says:

> One should repeat the mantra with confidence, faith, composure, regularity, certainty, contentment, enthusiasm, and qualities like these.[7]

And the *Bhagavad Gītā* joins constancy and one-pointedness, saying:

> He who thinks of Me constantly, whose mind does not ever go elsewhere, for this yogi who is constantly devoted, I am easy to reach, O Arjuna.[8]

In all these instances — and there are many, many more — constancy is seen as a virtue that enhances spiritual practice and leads to the attainment of the spiritual goal. It determines the success or failure of spiritual pursuits. Constancy is a beautiful virtue.

One day King Akbar put on a disguise and rode through his capital to see how his subjects were doing. As he rode toward a gold mine near the outskirts of the city, he saw a man sifting sand by the side of the path. The king dismounted and asked, "My dear fellow, what are you doing?"

The man said, "This is not mere sand. There are gold particles mixed in here, so I sift the sand. When I find the gold particles, I sell them. This is my livelihood."

The king felt great pity for this man, who was working so hard for a few particles of gold that he might or might not find. While the king was still standing beside him, the man went back to his sifting; he was intent on his task.

When the man wasn't looking, the king removed one of his precious gold bracelets, threw it on the mound of sand, and rode away. The next day, the king rode on the same path. Once again he saw the man sifting sand. He couldn't believe his eyes! He said, "My dear fellow, I heard a rumor that yesterday you found a beautiful precious gold bracelet. It was worth a lot. You could sell it and have enough money to take care of yourself and your family for the rest of your life. Why are you still here?"

The man smiled at the kind stranger, not knowing he was the king, and said, "My dear sir, I do this work constantly. Because I do it constantly, yesterday my efforts bore fruit, and I received a beautiful golden bracelet studded with jewels. Who knows? If I keep at it, I may receive something that is worth even more. So I must be constant at this."

In the same way, be constant in your practice of enthusiasm. Like the great saint Brahmananda, pray:

O Lord,
Allow me to know Your throbbing in my heart.
Let me always remember
You are the one who is throbbing in my heart.
Please show me Your true nature.
Show me Your true form.[9]

This great jewel of constancy, this practice of conforming to regularity, must be applied to both spiritual and worldly activities. Understand, it is not a question of becoming rigid or inflexible. This constancy is *nirantara*, it flows like a stream. And when it flows, you can experience an abundance of oxygen. You can drink from its flowing waters. There is a sweet flow of energy in constancy.

Constancy is like a boat moving steadily and surely toward its destination. There may be storms and strong winds that churn the surface of the sea, making you feel queasy. You may feel you don't want to go on; nevertheless, the boat keeps moving forward. Sometimes you may feel lazy or obstinate, or you may experience other limitations that are not so conducive to working beautifully or hard, or working well with other people. Nevertheless, the boat continues toward its destination.

Progress may not always be even. There may be setbacks. Still, the vessel moves through the changing tides, over the undulating waves. Whatever you undertake and wish to carry to a successful conclusion must be imbued with the brilliance of this jewel of constancy. Think of constancy as a jewel with many facets and great brilliance. This jewel will reveal itself to you in many aspects of your life as time goes on. You will experience the fruits of constancy when you are engaged in your paperwork, when you are writing an inspired article, or while sustaining your enthusiasm to meditate. You will notice the brilliance of constancy when you are chanting God's name or responding to the inquiries that cross your desk. You will be aware of its luster when you are recognizing God's presence in other people, when you are paying your bills, or while speaking respectfully to someone on the phone.

Being filled with enthusiasm and singing God's glory doesn't separate you from so-called worldly life. In fact, your daily tasks can awaken even greater enthusiasm within you and encourage you to sing God's glory. The inspiration that this message provides must flow through all your activities. In this way, it will purify and strengthen the core of your being so you can stand firmly in your belief, so you can fully embrace the Truth blazing within you.

In his book *From the Finite to the Infinite*, Baba Muktananda quotes the poet-saint Tulsidas, who says that when a river flows and flows continuously, eventually it merges into the ocean and becomes the ocean. In the same way, a person whose love for God is constant merges into God and becomes God.

The jewel of constancy shines in every cell of your body. Each cell constantly regenerates itself. Become aware of God's constant love for you. Become aware of the constant love that throbs in your heart. The fruit of the jewel of constancy is to be filled with enthusiasm and sing God's glory. Accept this jewel of constancy. Don't let it become a dusty heirloom. Actually wear it all the time. Learn to see God's glory in everything, everywhere.

Make this right effort constantly. It is a spiritual practice, it is sadhana. Remember: constancy is an inherent part of your nature.

With great respect, with great love, I welcome you all with all my heart.

*Sadgurunāth mahārāj kī jay!*

*Chapter 8*

# Patience, the Vitalizing Power of Enthusiasm

With great respect, with great love, I welcome you all with all my heart.

For a while now, you have been looking deeply into your own hearts to discover the source of enthusiasm. This is a wondrous sadhana. You can sense your capacity for enthusiasm expanding and expanding. There is great revelation when you look deeply into your intentions and discover the ability to sing God's glory nestling in your own heart.

As you contemplate what it means to be filled with enthusiasm, you realize that you cannot remain on a superficial level. You have to experience the sweet power of enthusiasm flowing from deep within in order for it to dance in your life. And there is so much to learn before this experience becomes tangible and constant. For instance, to sing God's glory is to appreciate everything in God's creation. So to begin with, you must accept everything that God provides for you: the pleasant and the less pleasant, the difficult and the less difficult — everything. You cannot bargain with God saying, "I'll sing Your glory, I'll be filled with enthusiasm if You give me all the good things — and all the bad things, give them to my enemies." No, you cannot bargain with God like that. You have to understand the true value of God's generosity.

Of course, it is a matter of great good fortune to experience enthusiasm for everything in life and to have the strength to sing God's glory. Nevertheless, you cannot forget that enthusiasm is also the fruit of your sadhana, and that sadhana is an ongoing process. You want to perceive God's light in everything all the time; that is the experience from which enthusiasm comes. To attain that, your sadhana must ripen and mature.

There is a spiritual practice that will help you enormously in reaching your goal. It is very subtle. It is essential. It is patience.

In the scriptures, patience is given a lofty position. Many related qualities are also invoked and praised: forbearance, endurance, fortitude, tolerance. These priceless qualities, which come to you during the course of your sadhana, have been honored by yogis down through the ages. They are the resources you must cultivate for your spiritual attainment. They are the true wealth you need in your sadhana. They are also the attainment in themselves.

When you look into each one of these terms, you see that they all have slightly different shades of meaning: forbearance, restraint in the face of obstacles; endurance, the ability to last, to survive hardships and adversity; fortitude, mental and emotional strength, the ability to withstand temptation; and tolerance, a form of stamina that keeps you from breaking down under the stresses and strains of spiritual growth. Yet for all the subtle differences among them, these terms have one thing in common: they represent different aspects of patience. If there is one great lesson to be learned in this world, it is patience.

Please understand, from the spiritual point of view patience is not about grinding your teeth and waiting for the most opportune moment to spring into action. It is not about standing still like a hunter waiting for the prey to come into range. Patience is not about biding your time until your wishes can be fulfilled. All these perspectives have given patience a very unappealing reputation. If anyone is a bit restless and demands something, he is told, "Be patient!" If someone speaks a mile a minute and tries to drive a point home, she is told, "Be patient!" If a child starts whining for a candy bar or begins to irritate his mother, he is told, "Be patient!" For all these reasons and more, patience has become associated with some kind of disturbance, an irritation. People even tell themselves to be patient when they themselves start acting up. They say, "Be patient! Just repeat the mantra. *Om Namah Shivāya, Om Namah Shivāya.*"

But patience is not just another way of saying, "Calm down" or "Be quiet." It is not a euphemism for these things. When you use it that way, it doesn't give you any room to analyze what is really going on inside. What are the deepest issues that you are trying to stifle in the name of patience? Why do you think and behave a certain way? Why do you seem to lose your temper? What makes you periodically break off your spiritual practices? When you keep hearing, "Be patient, be patient, be patient," you think the right thing to do is to shut down and wait it out until something better happens. Can this be why the scriptures, the saints, and the sages praise patience? No, I don't think so.

All these wrong ideas about patience keep you from appreciating the real value of this great quality, this extraordinary practice. If you think of patience as a consolation prize or a recipe for revenge, you will never be able to cultivate the virtue to its fullest. The fact is that patience truly makes you stronger. Patience is a noble quality. Think about it. Does patience really mean suppressing your freedom and strength? Does patience mean confining your thinking power within borders that are narrow and tame? Does patience mean subjugating your own wisdom and good sense to the opinion of others? Does patience mean letting others trample through your life? Does patience imply letting people get away with everything? Is patience the last resort of the weak and the passive? Is being patient the same thing as underestimating your own courage? Obviously, the answer is no.

Patience is an inner expression of great freedom and great strength. Patience is the vitalizing power of enthusiasm. It is part of what makes it possible for you to sing God's glory. It gives you time to recognize God's presence in this universe. Therefore, it is worthwhile taking a longer look at what patience is all about on the spiritual path so that you may learn to use it in a profitable manner. It is a great virtue, a wonderful practice.

What is patience? Baba Muktananda explained it by speaking from his own experience: "I had full faith in my Self and in God. Patience is very much connected with discipline, and patience results from deep faith in God, from the awareness that I am God's and God is mine, that He will not forsake me in any situation, that He will always protect me and guide me. For patience, what you need is faith in your own Self."

To hear Baba say that patience is the result of deep faith is so beautiful. It is connected to faith in your own Self, faith in God. Patience takes on a whole different meaning when we connect it to an even greater spiritual quality. Faith is so beautiful in itself. It reminds us that patience stems from a noble realm. It arises from deep within the heart. It is not a tool that you use to reprimand others or to get your own way. Patience is an essential part of the process of coming close to God. Patience is not a superficial mental construct. Not at all.

Baba also said that patience is very closely connected to discipline. So in order to attain patience you must practice it with great diligence. It is the product of a very refined awareness. Of course, when Baba uses the word *discipline*, he is referring to spiritual practices that are performed daily, with constancy. For example, in Siddha Yoga, we have daily meditation and chanting, *swādhyāya* (the recitation of the *Guru Gītā* and other sacred texts) contemplation, and service. So when Baba speaks of discipline, most of the time he is referring to these spiritual practices that are performed regularly, that allow purification to take place both within and without. This discipline is not a set of rules and regulations that have been laid down by just anyone. They are the advice of the sages and yogis who have followed them and attained the highest goal of life. Such discipline is essential for any seeker who is interested in making spiritual progress.

Patience, then, is a quality that matures inside a seeker. In India, whenever you see great patience in a little child, you say, "Oh, he is just like an old man" or "She is just like an old woman," and it is actually a compliment. I know it's different in other countries, but in India, when you call someone old, it means that he or she is very mature, seasoned in life. It's a great compliment. When you say a child is like an old man, that means his understanding has matured, there is patience in him. He has developed this beautiful quality within himself. So patience is a quality that matures in a seeker. It comes from understanding that is fully baked. It is a result of great discipline and deep faith in God. These are also qualities that must be practiced if they are to be attained.

Once there was a noble seeker who was traveling in search of his Guru. He had practiced austerities and various forms of yoga for a long time. But he could see that his attainment did not match that of the great yogis. He knew he needed the grace of a Master. He felt incomplete within. The most legendary Guru of that time was Gorakhnath. He was practically mythical. People said he had lived for hundreds and hundreds of years. This seeker had decided that he would settle for no other Guru but Gorakhnath. Of course, Gorakhnath was not easy to find. He was famous for wandering from one end of India to the other, appearing and vanishing at will. For years on end the seeker roamed in search of him.

One day, as he was walking along, he saw a striking yogi coming toward him. He was so luminous, so splendid. The seeker could tell from the man's bearing, and by the way his own heart began to pound so strongly, that this was a very high being. When they met, the seeker bowed before him.

The yogi asked, "Who are you? Where are you going? What do you want from me?"

"I am looking for Gorakhnath, my Guru."

The yogi smiled and said, "I am Gorakhnath."

The seeker was delighted. He prayed, "Please accept me as your disciple. Give me initiation. Make me yours. I'll go with you wherever you go. I'll do whatever you ask me."

Gorakhnath looked at this disciple and said, "Good. Now sit here until I return."

Gorakhnath was known for his wanderings, and it was possible he might not return for a long, long time. Still, the seeker followed the instruction — he was ripe within. He did not just sit there waiting like a rock; he did not shut down his inner being. He remained there with enthusiasm and opened his being to divine alchemy. He sat holding in his heart the power of his meeting with the Master. He allowed the silent thunder in the Master's voice and the secret lightning in his eyes to suffuse and transform his entire being. He did not become impatient and wander off before the process was complete.

After many, many long years had gone by, Gorakhnath passed that way again. Even before he returned, the disciple had become enlightened. But still, he continued to wait for his Guru. He had been told, "Sit here until I return." By following that one command, the disciple had attained full knowledge of his own Self. His dynamic patience had borne the highest fruit.

This is the true spirit of embracing patience on the spiritual path.

Let us look at patience from yet another angle. The great poet-saint Kabir once said:

> After all, this body is going to end up in the dust,
> so why do you go about with so much pride?
> O sadhus, listen to what Kabir says:
> Keep waiting for the Lord.
> You will find Him in your patience.
> Keep waiting for the Lord.
> You will find Him in your patience.[1]

Kabir's words hit very close to home. "This body is going to end up in the dust," he says. It is not a matter of speculation, not something that you can put off thinking about. You cannot say, "Oh, this doesn't concern me. I have plenty of time to deal with all this." That is no way to exercise patience. There must be urgency in your quest.

The point Kabir is making is this: why do you wander around so pridefully when the destiny of the body is so precarious? Kabir is dealing with a great paradox — the intertwining of urgency and patience. He says: Hurry up. You don't have much time. You never know when you will die. Hurry up! And in the same breath he says: "You will find God in your patience." It is a paradox. The teachings of the great ones are filled with paradoxes, and that is how they must be. This world is composed of pairs of opposites, and the way to deal with them is through paradox.

According to Kabir, then, you must hurry up — but have patience. When it comes to temporal matters, he infuses you with urgency. He refuses to listen to your excuses: "Well, I really can't go this fast. I have to wait until my grandchildren are old enough." No. He says: You have no time; don't get stuck in worldly matters.

What are these worldly matters? Pettiness, confusion, quarrels, wasting your time on insignificant things, wasting your energy. Don't postpone your spiritual practices. Absorb yourself in them right away. Don't put off being good to others. When it comes to being kind to others, be kind right away, this very minute. Stop dwelling on the pride of your own body. Drop your attachment to the worldly things that take you far away from remembrance of God. Remove yourself from that which is perishable. All this is urgent. Do it right now.

But then on the other hand, Kabir says: "You will find the Lord in your patience." Be patient in receiving His grace. Practice patience in experiencing His love. When the Lord comes looking for you, be available. Become anchored in tranquility. Waiting for the Lord is not just biding your time. It is actually a way of keeping His company.

The *Shrīmad Bhāgavatam* speaks about keeping the company of the Lord through constant remembrance. This is the best way to keep the company of God: constant remembrance of Him. You are filled with enthusiasm knowing you will see Him, knowing you will have the darshan of the Lord — in your dreams, as you chant, as you offer your service. You have the feeling "I will see the Lord, I am seeing the Lord." You sing His glory to please Him to the utmost.

Patience is also one of the subtle measures of the maturity or immaturity of a seeker. In ancient times there were two seekers who were doing their sadhana under a beautiful neem tree. It was a huge tree with countless green leaves. One day the celestial sage Narada passed by. The seekers greeted him most respectfully and listened gratefully as he sang a beautiful *bhajan*. Then they politely asked him where he was going.

As it happened, Narada was going to have the darshan of the Lord, and when they heard where he was going they asked if he would do them a favor. Narada was happy to agree. The seekers had a burning question: "Please ask the Lord when will our practices bear fruit? How soon will we attain liberation?"

Narada promised to ask the Lord on their behalf and he went on his way. Never had these two seekers prayed as intensely as they did now. Before long, Narada reappeared with the answer to their question. A direct message from the Lord Himself!

The first seeker was told that he would achieve his goal in twelve years. Just twelve years!

Hearing this, the seeker's smile faded. The light went out of his eyes. "Twelve more years! Under this tree? I can't bear it!"

It was too much to ask, too long to wait. By then he would be an old man with a face full of wrinkles. So he got up and walked away from the neem tree, leaving behind his austerities, leaving behind all his spiritual practices. He was going to enjoy the world after all. As a result, his sadhana went into a deep sleep, and he gained nothing from it.

Then Narada looked hesitantly at the second seeker. He approached him, took his arm, and said gently, "You will gain Self-realization after as many lifetimes as there are leaves on this neem tree." Narada took a deep breath and waited to see how the second seeker would react. As he waited, he looked up into the neem tree with its thousands of scintillating leaves.

Much to Narada's amazement, the seeker danced for joy. His eyes were shining like the stars. "I'm going to be liberated! I'm going to be enlightened! This is such divine news!" He could hardly contain himself and, grabbing Narada's arm, he cried out, "My quest has not been in vain! I'm going to be enlightened!"

This seeker redoubled his efforts; he intensified his practices. He increased his enthusiasm; he quickly went through many, many, many births and attained liberation.

Baba Muktananda found endless ways to encourage seekers to do sadhana. Whatever question you asked, Baba always had an uplifting answer. Yet the essence of all his answers was the same — meditate. So sweetly and so emphatically he would say, "Meditate, just meditate. Do your sadhana. Have faith." At one point Baba said, "It's not your fault if you want to go fast in meditation, but meditation is meant for a patient, steady mind. Meditation means that you apply brakes to your mind. It doesn't mean taking the brakes off and letting your mind race around at top speed."

Why don't you take a minute now and ask yourself some interesting questions: Why do you lose your patience? What makes you lose patience with yourself? With your body? With other people? With situations? Why do you lose patience in your seva? In your daily work? With your family members? What makes you lose patience with your sadhana? Why and when does your search for the Self start to look like something that is taking too long? Could it be that you have a specific timetable in your mind? Could it be that you have certain preconceived notions about how long things should really take? Ideas that are really wishes in disguise?

In the case of the body, for example, perhaps you have decided how fit you would like to become in a certain period of time, or that you would like to have mastered a certain hatha yoga posture by next week. Or you may have decided that you will always speak very sweetly no matter what, and you have given yourself exactly three days to achieve this. Perhaps you decided exactly how long it would take you to weed the garden or drive to the ashram or achieve a certain goal in life. You decided all this in advance. And when your expectations weren't met, when your desires were thwarted for one reason or another, you lost your patience. Seeking a specific goal, attaching yourself to a certain desired fruit — isn't that what provokes impatience? When a desire is frustrated, patience is lost.

The *Bhagavad Gītā* tells us again and again, unfulfilled desire leads to anger. It is such a simple teaching but so profound. No matter how much you contemplate this truth — an unfulfilled desire leads to anger — it is so difficult to master. And perhaps that is what is most disagreeable about impatience — its attachment to desire and its kinship with anger.

To remind oneself continually of the greatness of patience is an act of patience in itself. Patience is used to cultivate patience. Haven't you noticed when you rush to get things done, it always takes twice the time? When you rush to get the words out of your mouth, they always get tangled up and it takes twice the effort and twice the time to make them clear. When you rush to get somewhere, you sprain your ankle. When you rush to solve a problem, you create complications. When you rush to form an opinion about someone, you reveal a side of yourself that you usually keep hidden. That's one thing impatience does — it lets the cat out of the bag! For all these reasons and more, the wise person has always glorified patience and mistrusted haste.

When you are rushing just to get something over and done with, you sacrifice the beauty of the process. Isn't it patience that allows you to savor all the subtleties and fine points of your endeavors? When a task is executed with patience, doesn't it become more meaningful? When you are patient in your spiritual practices, don't you have many more great insights? Don't the practices begin to speak to you and reveal their mysteries?

When you exercise patience, you are giving something its due respect and allowing it to develop in its own time at its own pace. You cannot make a four-year-old child act like a forty-year-old adult. Sometimes parents complain that their young children are so full of mischief. If children can't be mischievous at four, when can they be? Right now is their time to play. So patience is allowing things to unfold in a more magnificent way than you are able to foresee.

To be wise and slow to anger is essential on the spiritual path and in the world at large. If you truly want to make spiritual progress, then patience is a supremely advisable habit to foster. The beauty of the words of the great beings and sages is that they make you aware that magnificent qualities like patience are inherent within you. You must learn to bring them forth from within. Patience is not something you acquire on the outside and wear like an ornament. You allow this jewel to emerge out of your own being and shine forth. The capacity for patience resides within you. All you have to do is learn to put it to good use. This is the greatest thing about the virtues. As you put them to good use, they grow more quickly, and you enjoy their fruits even more fully.

If you truly want to experience enthusiasm coursing through your body, if you truly want to have the awareness of God's glory turning all your words and actions into hymns of praise, then practice patience. Learn to put your patience to good use. Uncover this dynamic quality in the depths of your own heart. Nourish it with prayer and deep contemplation until its steady light radiates from the cave of your heart and penetrates all your subtle systems. Then, when it rises to the surface, it can be expressed in your actions.

Let your patience fill you with enthusiasm. Each time you feel a thought formulating in your mind, take a deep breath. Each time you are about to speak, take a deep breath. Give yourself time. Give yourself this gift. When you are speaking to someone and the conversation starts running away with you, take a deep breath. Take time. Don't be afraid of silence. Don't try to fill up the pauses.

Each time you are about to leap into action, give yourself a reward: take a deep breath and give yourself time to become comfortable, and then proceed with whatever you have to do. It is very important that you experience your own comfort, so make yourself comfortable before you speak. Before you perform any action, become comfortable with yourself; take the full support of your own being. It is all right to be concerned with yourself in this way; you are actually expressing unselfishness. You are taking time to gain the support of your entire being so that you can be more helpful to others. This is an expression of your own enthusiasm.

You truly do have all the time in the world. On the other hand, you can't afford to wait for patience to come to you on its own. You must learn to control the climate in which your thoughts and actions grow. If you want to go deep into meditation and realize its wondrous fruits, allow yourself to experience patience. Patience, as Baba said, is faith; it is forbearance; it is discipline. Remember, you don't make the sun rise by your will. You make yourself available and wait for the sun to rise. Then you drink in its beauty. In the same way, you cannot make the experience of meditation arise in your heart by force. You wait for it to happen. You wait patiently. And then you can bathe in its nectar, the sweet nectar of meditation. Then you can be filled with enthusiasm and sing God's glory.

With great respect, with great love, I welcome you all with all my heart.

*Sadgurunāth mahārāj kī jay!*

# Chapter 9

# Forgiveness Sings the Glory of the Heart

With great respect, with great love, I welcome you all with all my heart.

When you dive deeply into your own heart, what do you truly feel? Do you find your own bubbling enthusiasm? When you let your soul shine forth and fill everything around you with its brightness, how free do you feel? When you reveal all the enthusiasm within you, how taintless is it? When you sing God's glory, how freely does it resonate? When you walk on a forest path, how lighthearted are you? When you see the profusion of color in a summer garden, delicate and flamboyant at the same time, how tender does it make you feel? How close do you feel to nature? Do you allow nature to affect your heart?

The other day someone shared with me that for a long time he had been doing seva with modern machines. He was always reading magazines about new technology. Recently, his seva changed and he began to work in the garden. It was all so new to him, weeding the grass and looking at the leaves and pruning the plants. All of a sudden he found that when he was having lunch at home, he would look out the window and admire the leaves on the trees and the clouds in the sky and the butterflies and the hummingbirds. He hadn't even known they existed before. As he began to watch them with new eyes, his heart began to feel different. He was becoming aware for the first time of his true heart. It is so amazing how one day you wake up and you see the universe. You see with *shiva drishti*, the outlook of Shiva, the great Lord.

When you go to the Temple and have the darshan of Bhagawan Nityananda, how alone are you with him? How close do you feel to him? Can you hear him speak to you? Can you see him looking at you? Can you feel him breathing? When you sit for meditation, how empty is your heart of all burdens? When you think of the world at large, what is your opinion of it? When you think of the life you have been leading, how does it appear to you? How do you represent it in your mind's eye? What do you dwell on? Can you say you are carefree and sure of your own Self? Can you say you have great faith in God and gratitude for your spiritual life? Can you say your heart is totally at peace, completely free, and surrendered to God's will?

One day, Saint Francis was working in his garden digging up the earth and pulling out weeds. He was going about it with great vigor. He was very focused. Someone nearby asked him what he would do if he were to learn that he was going to die that evening. He replied, "I would finish hoeing my garden." Saint Francis had a light heart, completely free and at peace.

When you don't store grudges inside you, when you don't hang on to irritation with other people's behavior, when you don't hoard frustration over situations beyond your control, then you experience lightheartedness. You can actually believe in ecstasy. You can have faith in joy. Tranquility flows through your system. There is nothing to stop it, nothing to snag it, nothing to dam it up.

What is the power that allows you to experience enthusiasm like this in its fullness? What gives you the ability to sing God's glory without anything or anyone preventing it? What is the benevolent power that washes away ill will and maintains the sanctity of the chamber of the soul? It is forgiveness. So simple. To have enthusiasm and to feel free enough to sing God's glory, your nature needs to be filled with the attitude, the inner posture, of continual forgiveness. As long as you are unable to forgive both yourself and others, you are unable to recognize the profound love that dwells in the heart.

One who can forgive easily is able to experience divine beauty everywhere. Such a person revels in the beauty of a garden. He has room to take it in. Such a person can experience the silence of a country path. His mind is quiet enough to perceive, experience, and rejoice in the dynamic stillness of nature around him. Next time you are in a quiet place of nature, listen to the dynamic stillness around you. And listen to the dynamic stillness that exists within yourself as well.

All this comes naturally to one who forgives. It also comes to one who has been forgiven. Praying for forgiveness from the Lord is a form of worship that comes naturally to every human being. People want to be forgiven in order to move on, so they turn to the One whose forgiveness is unfailing.

The *Shiva Mānasa Pūjā*, a wonderful hymn from the tradition of Shankaracharya, is a good example of this form of prayer. One verse says:

> O Shiva, forgive all the mistakes that I have committed
> with hands or feet, with ears or eyes,
> with words or body, with mind or heart.
> O great Lord, forgive my transgressions,
> those past and those that are yet to come.[1]

Praying in this way the devotee opens his mind, his heart, and his soul completely. He wants to receive forgiveness, so he invites God's light to pour through him. With such prayer, the devotee is able to accept his own faults and turn them over to God. In doing so, he erases all sense of separation between himself and the One he worships. Prayer itself becomes the purifying force. It takes the devotee deep into his own heart, deep into his own soul, where he finds immense peace and the absolution of sins and faults. He feels God's grace flowing through his entire being, and he knows without a doubt that his prayer has been answered.

At one time or another, most people have gone down on their knees and completely surrendered themselves to the divine Power, completely undone themselves before God. Every devotee in the world knows what a freeing experience this is — to give yourself to the Lord with all your might. You are so absolutely free that you are able to drink the ambrosia of the heart and live from that space of pulsating energy. Filled with enthusiasm in the presence of God, you are able to appreciate the sweetness and the kindness that always surround you. Therefore, the poet-saint Brahmananda says:

> O Lord, may I always remember You in my own heart.
> Be merciful and show me Your true form.
> After forgiving a thousand lifetimes of shortcomings
> and misdeeds,
> help me to stay at Your feet.
> O Lord, keep me at Your feet.
> Be merciful. Show Your compassion to me.[2]

God's compassion is unfathomable, and yet somehow we do comprehend it. We understand that His compassion can eradicate the most tenacious, the darkest of sins. If an impurity is too hardened to dissolve, God's love simply washes it away. God's comforting hand can soothe a burning heart. But what about you? Are *you* able to forgive? Can *you* forgive yourself? Are you able to forgive others? If someone has hurt you badly, can you forgive such a person? And do the words "I forgive you" suffice? What about your thoughts? What about your feelings? Do you secretly hold on to grudges and memories, or do you let go? What does it really mean to forgive?

And even if you are able to forgive, does that mean the other person will never hurt you again? Is there a guarantee that this person will never take advantage of you again? Does it mean you are supposed to present yourself as a victim and live that way forever? Just where do you draw the line, and how?

The *Mahābhārata* says that forgiveness is one of the eight paths of dharma. It is a great virtue. Someone once asked Baba Muktananda: "Should we forgive a person for his fraud and cunning in order to cultivate forbearance in ourselves, or should we retaliate?"

Baba replied: "You should not retaliate, but at the same time you should keep your forgiving nature well concealed. Sometimes forgiveness has bad consequences. It is good to be forgiving but that must not encourage a perverse attitude in yourselves and others."

Baba's answer is very thought-provoking and deserves to be contemplated deeply. When you really look into your own heart, you begin to live from a place that is sacred and very pleasing to God. This place has to be protected at all times. Often people say that after chanting the name of God, or after meditating, their heart is open and they feel vulnerable. It is important that you protect this openheartedness, that you protect the sanctity of your own heart. You don't want to close down your heart just because you think the world is vicious. If you close down your heart, you deprive yourself of drinking the heart's ambrosia, of experiencing the ecstasy of God. Therefore, your openheartedness must be protected. To be forgiving you must be very strong as well; you must be able to stand firm in your true beliefs.

The ability to extend complete forgiveness does not come quickly or easily. It is a great virtue that must be cultivated for a long time. You need to understand what forgiveness is truly all about. So listen carefully.

When you offer your pure forgiveness, it does not replace the need for repentance to arise in the heart of the other person. True forgiveness is not like giving candy to a crying baby so that he will stop crying. Just because you are able to forgive someone does not obviate their need to confront their misdeeds. They must do their own inner work. Forgiveness is not putting a warm blanket over someone and saying, "It's okay. Really it's okay." No. Each person must go through the fire of repentance.

And repentance, understand, is not about sobbing like a wounded victim or telling the whole world your sad story. Repentance is a deep — a very, very deep — contemplation. It is entering the *sanctum sanctorum* of your own soul, going deep inside where no one else has access but you and your own God. Not even your closest friend, your most loved one, can go there. There is a place inside you that is pure, sacred, tranquil. Only you and your God can go there, and no one else has access to this innermost chamber of your soul. If your forgiveness prevents or short-circuits the other person's repentance, their deep contemplation, then it is not pure forgiveness. It is complicity. Of course, the one who forgives also has to give up something — the feeling of being victimized by the person who has done something harmful.

You have to look at the role you have played in the cycle of resentment. To be forgiving, you must have the courage to look at your thoughts, feelings, and deeds, and the consequences they create. Then you must firmly resolve to walk through them — not to blind yourself and not to hang on to them either. You do have to have the power to let go. You surrender them to God. So forgiveness does not replace repentance. It does not just wipe away the tears. Yet without the gift of forgiveness, repentance is not complete. This applies whether you are forgiving another person or forgiving yourself.

Now, what does it mean to be forgiven? Does it mean you have the license to go on doing whatever you want? You make mistakes and you say, "God, forgive me," and keep on going? Does it mean you are no longer required to give up the things that are detrimental to you and to the society you live in? The obvious answer is no. The way to receive forgiveness is to accept it as a turning point in your life. It should turn you around and set you on a better path. Only then have you truly accepted forgiveness, only then have you truly given forgiveness.

True forgiveness opens the path of light. It brings you closer to God, to your own heart. It helps you to experience the love of your own heart. This is true both for the one who is forgiven, as well as for the one who forgives. Like all the noblest virtues, forgiveness creates a blessed atmosphere in which all the other great qualities of your Self shine forth. When you offer forgiveness, there should be no implicit contract: "I forgive you if you do this for me. I forgive you if you promise that every day you will smile at me." That would take away your enthusiasm because you would not be free. You are expecting something to happen, and the deal does not always come through. And even if it does, and you receive what you want, you are still stuck in the conditions of a deal.

Forgiveness is a great blessing, not just to receive but also to give. And in a certain way, it is also the only wise choice. The alternative is much too dark. As the poet-saint Kabir says:

> If someone abuses you once
> and you react by abusing him,
> then his one abuse becomes two.
> However, if you do not abuse him in return,
> one abuse remains only one.[3]

This is beautiful advice — and hard to follow. To carry it out, you must have great strength of heart and the strength that comes from wisdom. If you do not participate in multiplying the offense, the affront, the ill treatment, the rudeness, the provocation, and the hurt, if you do not allow pain to pile up until it becomes like a mountain, you will not have to worry about how to climb over it. You can give yourself many other options. Forgiveness becomes harder and harder when you react to unpleasantness with more unpleasantness.

Unsavory modes of behavior are dangerous things to play with. When you forget that your thoughts create your world, you become careless. When you forget that your words create your future, you can be caught off guard. When you are trapped in certain situations, the temptation to strike back may be appealing — so appealing that you want to keep on striking back. You think you will feel lighter after that. But you forget the mountain of pain you are creating for yourself later on.

To forgive someone, you must have a very great heart indeed. But to avoid returning abuse with more abuse, to refuse to bite back, your heart must be even greater. Therefore, forgiveness is also a way of showing kindness to yourself and allowing yourself to recognize the greatness of your own soul. During a crisis, forgiveness is a true friend you can count on. In adversity, forgiveness is a great ally.

Forgiveness is a way of recognizing God's undeniable presence in your life. It is so easy to say, "God does not exist in my life all the time. There are times when God forgets about me." If you can remain close to your good nature and forgive, then you will also realize that God does not forget you even when you think He does. Only a forgiving heart can sing God's glory with total abandonment. Only a forgiving heart is able to pass through the tunnel of fire unscathed. You cannot avoid difficulties in this world. Nevertheless, you always have options about how you are going to face the difficulties. Remain constantly aware of the state of your own heart. Nurture the purity and the strength of forgiveness.

You have only so much time, and you do so many things in your life. You work, you cook, you take care of children, you go to parties. There is so much to do. However, just because you have all those things to do, you must not forget the state of your own heart. In everything you do, the state of your heart is very significant — not just how you feel or what your mood swings are, but how strong your heart is, how noble your heart is, how dharmic your heart is. Therefore, nurture the purity and strength of forgiveness.

The *Mahābhārata* tells us that forgiveness dissolves anger. It is so easy to feel angry with people who don't seem to fulfill your ideals. For example, it is much more convenient to be angry at your parents for falling short than it is to forgive them. It is easier to sit in a restaurant and vent your anger about the way others treat you than it is to forgive them. It is more comfortable to think of yourself as someone in a position to be displeased by others' inefficiency than it is to offer forgiveness.

Forgiveness is seated in the heart. When you are able to experience forgiveness, it carries all the other great qualities of the heart along with it. And yet even when you want to forgive, it's hard to let go of the addiction to anger. You see, you don't really have to worry about anger as such; it is the addiction to anger that is the problem. Somehow people think they have to become highly evolved and spiritually elevated before they can forgive their families, their co-workers, and their friends. Therefore, they neglect the presence of God in their own hearts, the presence of God that is shining so brilliantly. They think they have to become purer and greater to have the power to forgive. Therefore, they don't even want to think of truly forgiving, even though the people they are angriest with are often the people they are closest to and love the most, even though an unforgiving attitude hurts them more than anyone else.

How can you be filled with enthusiasm and sing God's glory if your heart is burning in the fire of anger, in the fire of negativities, if your heart is burning in the fire of total dissatisfaction? Forgiveness dissolves anger. Forgiveness is simple and its fruit is sweet. Forgiveness can be hidden amidst other expressions of goodness, such as kind words and unselfish actions. Forgiving others is not just saying to them, "I forgive you." Your actions also reveal forgiveness.

Whether your forgiveness is implied through your actions or clearly stated through your words and gestures, let the current of spontaneous, unconditional forgiveness flow in your own heart. Let it come through your heart; let it not be just a mental exercise. Allow your entire being to be involved in forgiving. If you can just go ahead and do it without waiting for some great event to occur, you will find yourself in paradise.

Remember, you cannot really forgive someone and still hang on to the memory of old grudges. Why? Because a beautiful alchemy takes place within the one who forgives and also within the one who is forgiven. So if you don't want to be finished with old grudges, if you're still attached to them, don't forgive. As soon as you forgive, the grudges will dissolve.

Sometimes people say, "Gurumayi, please give me just enough blessings to get through my problems, but don't take away my problems completely because without them I wouldn't know what to do." These people come with grave, serious faces, and if I make them laugh, they get really upset. They say, "Gurumayi, let me finish telling you about my sadness, my suffering. Don't make me laugh, please, because then I can't tell you." You really do need to watch out for your attachments to old memories.

Once you forgive, truly a great alchemy takes place within yourself, and you feel so free, so good. You can breathe deeply and really appreciate the leaves on the trees and the sunlight and the sweetness coming from people. You open yourself to grace, and then grace comes pouring into your life. Light comes pouring in, and you feel so expanded. You are suffused with a new energy that makes you feel greater and greater within yourself as your life unfolds.

You can talk about forgiveness, you can contemplate forgiveness, you can try to practice it. But in reality there comes a time when you don't really have to think about forgiveness at all. Forgiveness doesn't even occur to you because you have wisdom. You come from the space of wisdom.

Wisdom in its nature is forgiving, and therefore, if you have good understanding, forgiveness automatically takes place. You don't even have to think about forgiving, nor does the other person have to think about whether or not you have forgiven. It just happens. It just is. Where there is wisdom, where there is knowledge, forgiveness is not something you need to think about. You don't worry about whether you are going to receive forgiveness or offer forgiveness. Your very nature is wisdom, it is the fountain of knowledge.

You pray to the Lord saying, "O Lord, forgive me. Have mercy upon me." But think about God, the embodiment of wisdom. God is not sitting there waiting to punish you. You punish yourself with your own thoughts, your own deeds, the way you go about doing things, the way you deal with people and circumstances. You create punishment for yourself. The great Lord, as such, does not punish you. So truly speaking, the Lord does not have to forgive you. He is always merciful, always compassionate. He is the embodiment of wisdom. Where there is wisdom, forgiveness does not even arise. It is just there, as wisdom. If you have good understanding about something, your heart does not hold grudges. You feel completely free. You experience the truth of the situation. You experience greatness. It just is. So if you have wisdom, you know what forgiveness is all about. Forgiveness is inherent in wisdom.

Remember the innermost chamber of the soul, the place where only you and your God have access, the place deep inside. Remember to visit this place. That is where wisdom is. From there, knowledge springs forth. You will be filled with enthusiasm and sing God's glory.

Right now, for a few minutes, make a pilgrimage to this holy place of yours, the heart. Allow your awareness to become finer and finer. Remember a time when beautiful wisdom arose in your heart as someone was speaking to you nastily, angrily. How did you handle the situation? What was the state of your inner heart? Were you able to see that your own wisdom contained total forgiveness? Were you able to perceive the protection of this wisdom?

Allow yourself to reach the innermost chamber of your own soul. Come to this sacred place where only you and your God have access. How have you kept this sacred place? How does it shine? Meditate on this sacred space in the innermost chamber of your own soul. When you get in touch with your own divine power, you create paradise. Allow yourself to remember your own divinity within. Be filled with enthusiasm and sing God's glory.

With great respect, with great love, I welcome you all with all my heart.

*Sadgurunāth mahārāj kī jay!*

*Chapter 10*

# The Marvelous Balance of Gentleness

With great respect, with great love, I welcome you all with all my heart.

We have been looking at different qualities, different virtues, that help a person to be filled with enthusiasm and sing God's glory. We have also been looking at attributes that dampen your enthusiasm and remove the possibility of singing God's glory. We have examined the influence of self-hatred, the beauty of constancy, the value of patience, and the attainment known as forgiveness. For many people it is quite a revelation to see where they stand in relation to these qualities and how they are affected by them inside and out. As you examine closely the way you think, the way you feel, and the way you perform actions, you also notice the way all this creates your environment. As Baba Muktananda used to say, "Your thought creates your world."

The effects of this form of self-inquiry are delightful and intriguing; they are evocative and full of amazement. We are examining subjects that come up regularly in everyday life. They are quite familiar to everyone, and their very familiarity, their everyday commonness, often disguises the real power of these qualities. People tend to misunderstand, or they forget to understand, the real meaning of these words because they are used so often in daily conversation. When that happens, the terms lose their vibrancy and liveliness. They become banal. People grow accustomed to these words and take them for granted. They begin to think they know all about them, when, in fact, they have forgotten what the words truly stand for. These magnificent qualities are sometimes given connotations that are not so noble. People even make fun of them. "Oh," they say mockingly, "you're so virtuous." They tend to forget that these virtues come from a source of immense inner support. Our very being is the support of these virtues.

One of the astounding virtues is gentleness. In the time of the Vedas, gentleness was recognized as sacred. It was a blessing to be prayed for, it created an atmosphere you wanted to live in. On behalf of the community, the sages of the *Atharva Veda* pray:

> Grant us Your blessings
> that Mother Nature may be kind to us,
> that the heavens give us peace,
> that the Earth be gentle.
> Gentle be the waters that flow;
> gentle be the plants and herbs that grow.
> May the past be kind and the future benign.[1]

What kind of world do you want to live in? How do you want to behave with each other? In the *Shrīmad Bhāgavatam*, the sage says:

> May the world be peaceful.
> May the wicked become gentle.
> May all creatures think of mutual welfare.
> May their minds be occupied with what is auspicious.
> And may our hearts be immersed in selfless love for the Lord.[2]

Peace, mutual well-being, auspiciousness, selflessness, love — these are the qualities that accompany gentleness. Where there is gentleness, other virtues always appear as well.

Gentleness, or *mardavam* in Sanskrit, is one of the faces of God; it is one of the most benevolent expressions of grace. We are instinctively grateful when grace comes our way in a gentle manner. Sweet tears moisten our hearts when we experience that the nature of the Divine is gentle, it is *mridu,* it is *komala,* it is *saumya.*

Isn't there something incredibly touching about a gentle breeze? Doesn't your heart expand and grow still beside a gentle brook? What is the effect of a gentle rain, so soft, so mist-like? You linger, you want to stay there just a few more minutes in the graceful mist, the gentle rain. Think of gentle hills curving with woods and meadows, fragrant with wildflowers, filled with the delicate call of songbirds. Does anything melt your heart more than the gentle behavior of a child or a gentle word from a loved one?

Isn't gentleness always welcome? Has anyone ever complained to you that you are being so gentle they are sick of it? We are not talking about a syrupy quality or always trying your best to please others, but about true gentleness. This gentleness warms your soul and calms your heart in whatever form it comes. A gentle look from a tiger, the gentle rays of the morning sun, the gentle movement of an eagle gliding through the air. All these creatures and forces have the capacity to be fierce and tumultuous. Yet when they reveal their gentleness, your heart leaps up into ecstasy. When their aspect is so gentle, don't you rejoice? Don't you experience God's love? Doesn't your heart want to sing God's glory? When someone has been very tough with you for years and years on end and then one day shows gentleness to you, shows sweetness to you, don't you feel it was worth waiting for? A drop of nectar after the scorching sun — ah, such gentleness.

When the awakened Kundalini is gentle, when She works through you in a very gentle manner, how do you feel? Or think of the gentle call of a loved one or a gentle reminder from a friend. When someone corrects you gently, you say, "Oh, thank you. Every time I do that, please remind me." Or think of being gently encouraged to set out on the spiritual path. Or even the gentle rise and fall of flames in a hearth.

What is the effect of gentleness in all these cases? It removes fear. That's what really happens. When you are able to convey gentleness, when you are able to exhibit gentleness, when you are able to speak from gentleness, when you are able to act from gentleness, it removes fear. It removes fear in others, and it removes fear within yourself. It opens your heart. Gentleness allows you to trust and move forward. Gentleness relaxes your entire being so that you are able to appreciate the innate goodness of the universe. Unless you relax, you can't experience the goodness in this universe. Gentleness, tenderness, is what you seek in your innermost heart. When the whole pompous show is over, and you are all alone, what do you ask for? Gentleness. Sweetness. Tenderness. Not another wrestling partner. No, you want gentleness. When you are going through a hard time and you experience God's gentleness, you are filled with gratitude.

Although gentleness may assume the appearance of meekness, it is definitely not spineless. Gentleness may seem to be soft and delicate, but make no mistake about it, true gentleness cannot be taken advantage of. Gentleness may be moderate, tender, light, easy, and sweet, but none of this implies any lack of strength. Not at all. There is nothing helpless about gentleness. In fact, as a French saint says: "Nothing is so strong as gentleness, nothing so gentle as real strength."

Think about it. When you truly feel strong, don't you experience gentleness? You don't feel like showing off your strength. In fact, your gentleness shines forth. And when you are feeling very gentle, you don't feel weak, you feel strong, you feel all the gods and goddesses are by your side.

The privilege of experiencing gentleness and of being gentle comes to one whose faith is immense — faith in God's ways and faith in all that has already been achieved in one's inner life. I love to hear the mantra *Om pūrnamadah pūrnamidam* chanted. It means:

This is perfect, that is perfect,
everything is perfect.
When you take perfection from perfection,
what remains is perfection.
All this is perfect.[3]

Each time I hear this mantra chanted, I experience incredible gratitude and deep, deep satisfaction. It's such a great, gentle reminder. It's like a *dhāranā* that can be practiced all day long: "This is perfect, that is perfect." When someone speaks to you very sweetly: "This is perfect." When someone speaks to you not so sweetly: "That is perfect." When someone praises you: "This is perfect." When someone doesn't praise you, in fact, doesn't mind making you feel miserable: "That is perfect." When things go your way: "This is perfect." When things don't go your way: "That is perfect." When you feel healthy: "This is perfect." When you don't feel so healthy: "That is perfect." It's a great *dhāranā*.

Please understand, this is not a technique for making the mind or intellect numb so that you cannot think, or judge, or discriminate anymore. It is a means for extracting the perfection from each moment. God is perfect, this universe is perfect; therefore, perfection must be inherent in every particle of this universe. You may forget things, you may make mistakes, you may make blunders, you may do all kinds of things; yet that doesn't mean there is no perfection in God, there is no perfection in God's universe. It is your sadhana to extract the perfection from each moment, from each particle of the universe.

And how do you do that? You do it through contemplation, continuous contemplation. Instead of allowing the mind to enter into a negative mode and prattle away until it devours its own consciousness, its own nectar, you fill the mind with the words of the Siddhas, the words of the scriptures: *Om pūrnamadah, Om pūrnamidam*, "This is perfect. That is perfect." As you do that, incredible understanding blossoms. You are able to receive wisdom from your own inner being, from your inner fountain of knowledge. When you are gentle, you are able to extract this perfection. And you must be *truly* gentle; you cannot force it. If you force it, you lose it. When you are gentle, you are able to extract perfection from every particle of this universe.

Such gentleness is also great strength. This kind of strength is more than just physical strength. It is strength of heart, strength of mind, strength of understanding and experience, strength of contemplation and higher knowledge. When you are in trouble, when everything goes wrong in your life, when all your friends and relatives have left you, when it seems the whole world is against you, it is your knowledge that will give you support. That is the best company you can have. The strength of your knowledge is very important. It is one thing that will never leave you.

So the greater your knowledge, the gentler you are, because you continuously experience great humility in God's world. You are sobered again and again. And this being sobered is not humiliating at all. It is understanding that there is an even greater knowledge that you can access, that you can achieve. Whoever is the strongest is also the gentlest. This gentleness is full of strength and full of vigor, and it is totally fearless.

Near the end of an Intensive, someone once asked Baba Muktananda:

> I am one of the "wet logs" that takes a long time to ignite. This is my first Intensive, and nothing of apparent significance has happened yet. What are some possible explanations? What is the prognosis?

Baba's compassionate reply was this:

> It doesn't matter; the *shakti* will pursue you. You may not experience it for a month. It is all right if the log is wet, but your mind, your inner being, your faith, shouldn't be like a stone. That inner part should be soft. Then it's very

easy to dry up that log. The reason nothing happens to you is not because the body is a wet log; it is only because your mind, your faith, is like a stone. The *Bhagavad Gītā* says that the more faith you have, the sooner your inner being can be ignited. Faith is the magnet that pulls God toward you.

What Baba said is so beautiful, "That inner part should be soft." It is the softness of the heart that makes you sensitive to the Guru's grace. The softer your heart, the greater is your experience of the Guru's grace. Softness implies humility, tender love, yearning. Softness may also refer to knowledge of the scriptures, love for God's creation, compassion, the ability to understand other people's suffering. This softness, this gentleness of the heart is what manifests as faith: relying on God's grace, being part of God's family, accepting God's ways. If you allow yourself to become aware of the inner softness, you let faith blossom.

In the Jewish tradition it is said that a good rule for going through life is to keep the heart a little softer than the head; God conceals Himself from the mind of human beings, but reveals Himself to the heart. Such a sublime definition of gentleness: keeping the heart soft. Doesn't it take you to a higher consciousness when you hear what the great ones say about gentleness?

The gentleness you practice must not be fake. It is not a mask you put on to impress others. You cannot wear gentleness like that. It is not a disguise you put on and take off when you want to. Gentleness is not something you wear so that others will say, "Oh, what a pious person you are. You must be so pure."

Nor is gentleness a way to extract others' sympathy, to manipulate their feelings, or to take advantage of their good intentions. The gentleness that you must practice has nothing to do with a "poor me" attitude. You must understand one thing about Siddha Yoga: Baba never liked the "poor me" attitude. Never. He liked us to be strong. He liked us to follow his teachings. And he made it clear that when we served the "poor me" attitude, we were turning our backs on something higher, something much more beneficial than self-pity.

There is nothing limp about the divine quality of gentleness. In its true form it adorns your heart. It allows God's flame to shine brilliantly. It reveals God's generosity. It proclaims God's unconditional love for all. It improves the atmosphere around you and gives everyone you come in contact with greater hope and faith in humanity.

How can you distinguish between gentleness and false humility? It is so simple: by the way it makes you feel. There is something about the empty affectation of meekness that makes you feel uncomfortable, whereas gentleness creates enthusiasm. True gentleness gives birth to greater virtues. It is very important to make this distinction. Otherwise, gentleness becomes another costume for hypocrisy and pretension, and this ends up giving spiritual life a very questionable reputation. It makes the path to God look like the last refuge for people who cannot face the challenges of the world.

As a matter of fact, that's just what happened to a tiger. As a youngster, he had been the terror of the jungle — swift, daring, ferocious, with sharp teeth and a huge appetite. He had killed, plundered, and devoured to his heart's content. But one day the inevitable happened — he grew old. His teeth fell out. His reflexes slowed down and he could no longer move quickly. In short, he turned into a weak old cat that the slowest creature could outrun. The only thing that didn't diminish was his voracious appetite. He was hungry all the time, and he was afraid he might starve to death.

He thought to himself, "What can I do? I can't catch anything, so I've got to outsmart these animals. It's my only choice.

I know! I'll pretend to be gentle and nonviolent. I'll walk very slowly and blow away all the insects from under my feet. I'll go *puff . . . puff* as if I can't bear the thought of killing even a tiny insect. And then, if anyone comes to honor me for my gentleness and nonviolence, I'll get him! The most religious creatures are always the tastiest."

So he set out. First, he'd puff on the ground and then put one foot down. Then he'd puff again and put the next foot down, crying loudly, "*Hari Om tat sat! Om shānti shānti.*"

Before long, from high up in a tree, a monkey looked down and saw the amazing sight. "Look at that!" he thought. "Everything about that tiger is so gentle and spiritual — his beard, his eyes, his ears. He's become the embodiment of nonviolence." The little monkey was fascinated at the exquisite sight. He thought, "I'm getting old. I've never thought of God. All I've ever done is play. I should go to Tiger Baba and ask him for initiation."

Without another thought, the monkey scampered down the tree and sat meekly before Tiger Baba with folded paws. Tiger Baba closed his eyes. He was in silence. The monkey quietened his breathing so as not to disturb Tiger Baba's silence. Hours went by. The monkey thought it must be a test. He thought, "Tiger Baba is testing me to see if I'm a true seeker. If I am, then he'll give me initiation."

A whole night went by. Every now and then, the monkey could hear *Om shānti, Om shānti* going on in Tiger Baba's head.

"Ahh, he's even thinking the mantra. I must wait." But when morning came, the monkey was tired and cold. So he gathered up all his courage and in a very soft voice he said, "Tiger Baba, I think I'm ready for initiation."

Tiger Baba slowly opened his eyes. "*Hari Om tat sat. Om shānti shānti.*" He looked at the monkey. And the monkey felt incredible energy coming from the tiger. He just knew he was receiving initiation. He could feel his heart thumping and the energy moving through his body.

Gently, Tiger Baba said, "So be it. Receive initiation."

The monkey was so happy that he did a full *pranām* at Tiger Baba's wonderful, clawlike feet. Without wasting a second, Tiger Baba grabbed the monkey with his teeth.

No wonder the monkey's heart was pounding. No wonder he had felt such energy coming out of the tiger's eyes. "What a fool I am!" thought the monkey. "I must do something!" So he began to laugh and laugh.

Tiger Baba was nonplussed. He couldn't understand why the monkey was laughing, so he growled in confusion. The monkey, still caught in the tiger's mouth, said, "You don't know? You haven't heard? The whole jungle has been talking about it. I can't believe you haven't heard."

The tiger made another strange sound.

The monkey kept talking. "Let me tell you, Tiger Baba. Anyone who laughs very hard at this moment will go to heaven. That's why I'm laughing." And again the monkey began to laugh and laugh. When he finally stopped, he said, "Tiger Baba! You should laugh too. This is the moment. This is it! Laugh and you'll go to heaven!"

Tiger Baba thought, "I've been following the spiritual path — not just to eat. I think I do want to attain God, after all. And who knows, there may be nectarean creatures to eat in heaven. I should laugh." So Tiger Baba gathered up his courage and let out an uproarious laugh. The entire jungle echoed his laughter, as the monkey scampered up a tree.

There he began to cry very bitterly.

Tiger Baba was totally confused. "O monkey, I don't understand you. When you were in my teeth, you should have been crying, but you laughed. And now that you're free, you're crying. Tell me why."

"Tiger Baba, I'm talking to God as I cry. I'm asking Him why He sends creatures like you into this world — creatures like you that cannot be honest for a second, cannot be truthful for a second, cannot truly follow nonviolence even for a second. Why does God create beings like you? When I laughed, I was laughing at my own stupidity for trying to get something important without thinking about it first. And now I'm crying — crying about how many people will be deceived by you."

You cannot put on a mask of gentleness, a mask of humility. You cannot pretend your heart is soft. Sometimes very, very angry people fall in love and they say, "Oh, these days my anger is gone. My heart is so full of love; I'm experiencing love all the time." And then after a few hours, or a few days, or a few weeks, they are back to being their angry self. What happened? It was just a chemical reaction that created the apparent softness. Your inner being must be soft *underneath*; that's the softness Baba talks about. If softness doesn't exist in the inner part, you cannot pretend it is there. You cannot just don a cloak of nonviolence. But you can cultivate it. With good understanding, by being good to others, by studying the scriptures and serving humanity, you can cultivate it, and you can make it grow. This way you are filled with enthusiasm and singing God's glory.

In one of his *abhangas*, Tukaram Maharaj, the great poet-saint of Maharashtra, says:

> We are servants of the Lord.
> We are softer than butter
> and yet harder than a diamond.[4]

Baba once commented on this verse: "Tukaram Maharaj says, I am so tender, my heart has become so soft, that if I were to lie on a bed of flowers, I would get hurt. But at the same time, I'm so tough that I could break a thunderbolt to pieces."

Gentleness is strength, and strength is gentleness. It is an extraordinary statement, "We are softer than butter and yet harder than a diamond." In Baba Muktananda, these two virtues of gentleness and strength lived in great harmony. He was the embodiment of love, and he was the embodiment of discipline. He did not slacken in discipline because of love. His emotions never got in the way of exercising discipline in the ashram. He was able to show the direct, narrow path. When you hear these statements from great beings, how their hearts are softer than butter, softer than flower petals, yet they are very strong, you cannot consider them helpless victims of society. You begin to see the marvelous balance in gentleness between what you think of as soft and what you think of as strong. Your whole idea about what is soft and what is strong begins to shift. You have to adjust your understanding to this kind of softness and this kind of strength.

The softness here is not ephemeral. It is not like a dandelion that has gone to seed in a ball of fluff that the slightest breeze can scatter. Nor is the strength of gentleness like iron, cold and unbending. Gentleness never expresses itself frivolously. And it never manifests as mere lip service either. Sometimes people may really put you through the mill and then say, "Well, I don't know what you're complaining about; I'm really being very gentle with you." And you think, "Well, if this is gentleness . . ." Gentleness does not manifest through words alone. Either you are being gentle or you are not.

Softness of the heart is not the same as being naive. Softness is not gullible. And its strength never overrides the fruit of others' work. This is really all about maintaining a very fine balance. Sometimes you meet people whose behavior is very bossy, authoritative, and unkind. There is always a reason for such behavior. It may be that in order to make their way in the world, such people feel they have to be extremely assertive and let others know who is in charge. And sometimes they are afraid to experience the softness of their own hearts. They have so much love for others, they fear if they express it they will lose their identity, they will drown. So they try to contain all that love on the inside and act tough on the outside as well.

The expression of gentleness is about maintaining a very fine balance. You can't be too soft or too strong. You can't go too far to one side of the scale or the other. You want to bring about harmony and balance. You want to extract strength from gentleness and gentleness from strength. You need to maintain this kind of balance in other areas too. For example, understanding the worth of spiritual practices, and at the same time honoring all of God's creation; taking care of your daily duties and responsibilities, and at the same time remembering the highest principles of spiritual life.

Although Baba stressed the importance of cultivating gentleness, in no way did he ever condone being fainthearted or spineless. In Baba's eyes, you could be gentle and still refuse to be feeble. You could be gentle and still decline to be at the mercy of circumstances.

Gentleness naturally settles over a spiritual environment. When you walk into the Temple in Shree Muktananda Ashram, you naturally become very respectful. You don't dash into the Temple, *pranām* to the sandals, and pray in a hurry. And if you ever do, you must have noticed it creates great restlessness and agitation; it is as though something has really gone wrong. If your entire day is filled with restlessness and anxiety, you should go back to the moment when you first woke up or first meditated, first went to the Temple, first did your worship. Go back to that moment. You will realize it was then that you were forgetful, you were in a hurry.

It is very important to protect the sacred atmosphere of the moment when you wake up. Whether you meditate or do *pūjā*, repeat your mantra, think about the Guru, or glorify God — whatever worship begins your morning — that is the most important moment. And you can actually go back and redo it. You can do mental *pūjā*. Mentally, place yourself on your meditation *āsana*. If you usually put *bhasma* on your body, do that. If you wear *rudrāksha* beads, put them on. However you do your meditation and *pūjā*, take every step in your thoughts and do it with a very calm mind, giving full attention to each moment. It only takes a few minutes to perform this mental worship. You may have meditated for an hour and a half that morning, but if you were in a hurry it affected your entire meditation. This mental worship you can do for just five minutes very slowly. You will notice that all your restlessness disappears. Your entire being changes. Once again, you are back on track, and you feel that oneness with the universe, that oneness with God.

In a spiritual environment this gentleness naturally comes over you. In Gurudev Siddha Peeth, as we were growing up, we moved gently in the dormitories. Baba always emphasized that. We walked gently. We closed the doors gently. We spoke gently in the dormitories and in the gardens, and we put things down gently so as not to make clattering noises — not to disturb the God in others. As we tiptoed in and out of the Meditation Cave, we even breathed gently. I remember many times holding my breath as I entered and left the Cave, because I did not want to disturb anything. We learned to do everything gently so as not to disturb the sacred atmosphere. Of course, we didn't learn all this quickly and easily. Baba was always there reminding us.

When you pick up a little baby, you are very gentle. You don't thrust your hands forward and snatch it up. Nor do you grab at an article used in worship; you hold it very gently. You don't play catch with a fine crystal. Whenever you hold something precious in your hands, you are gentle with it. At the beginning of a new relationship, you are quite gentle as well. In every one of these cases, gentleness is a way of being careful, merciful, of showing how precious something is to you. You are actually acknowledging its greatness.

Gentleness, as you can see, is not such an unusual or otherworldly quality. Nonetheless, like anything else in this world, it must be looked after attentively and maintained and given space to expand. This is the greatest thing about the virtues: you can let them expand as much as possible. You can never say, "This is the limit." It is not as if you become the embodiment of gentleness, and there is no more room to grow. Just as you can't know the end of eternity, in the same way, you can't know the end of the virtues. There is always more room to grow.

If you don't guard gentleness, then you can become brittle. The *Tao Te Ching*, one of the sacred texts of Chinese mysticism, says:

> A man is born gentle and weak.
> At his death he is hard and stiff.
> Green plants are tender and filled with sap.
> At their death they are withered and dry.
>
> Therefore the stiff and unbending
> is the disciple of death.
> The gentle and yielding is the disciple of life.[5]

"Green plants are tender and filled with sap." Be filled with enthusiasm and sing God's glory. Maintain this liveliness in you, this great wonder, this freshness. Let rejuvenation happen every second of the day in your body, in your awareness.

What is the connection between gentleness and enthusiasm? We have been talking about enthusiasm for a long time now, and as you contemplate it more, your understanding becomes more subtle. You know that enthusiasm is not necessarily expressed in a loud voice. God's glory is often a gentle song. When enthusiasm courses through your being, you are full of life, full of love. You are also able to be sensitive to other people. You are able to invoke God's presence. And then, bathing in His unconditional love, you can abandon yourself to singing God's glory with total freedom. Let your enthusiasm be suffused with gentleness. Truly, it creates a beautiful world. Your mind is at peace. Your heart overflows. The clarity of your intellect is refined. Your heart is able to embrace the Truth, and the Truth is nectar. You feel revived.

With its quiet strength and steadiness, gentleness is difficult to ignore. Even pride gives way to gentleness. Pride that is oblivious to any need but its own and therefore shameless in its cruelty to others. Pride that is blind to others' goodness. Pride that only thinks about itself and is unsympathetic to anyone else's situation. Pride that is so easily upset, so quick to take offense, so reluctant to forgive. Pride that gathers like a dark cloud looming treacherously over your sense of mercy. If pride shuts you out and cuts you off, surrounding you with hard edges and brittle surfaces, what does gentleness do? It doesn't give up. Gentleness opens up both the outer and the inner worlds. So you can just imagine the access it gives you to the kingdom of God. Allow your enthusiasm to flourish in the light of gentleness. Then you will sing God's glory with your whole body, your whole mind, and your whole heart.

To learn about gentleness, you don't have to look too far, you don't have to withdraw from the world. Nature constantly gives lessons about this wonderful quality. Therefore, attune yourself in some way to the vibrations of nature. Follow the course of nature day by day. Watch the way the clouds tower in the sky on a sunny day. They carry the weight of an incredible quantity of water, yet they are completely light, hardly moving, like gossamer catching the light. Watch a flower open. Watch a gentle rain fall, penetrating deep into the soil, tenderly nourishing and sustaining life on this earth. Watch the moon at night. Notice the gentle way that moonbeams illumine and transform the landscape and make it magical, giving life to the herbs that sustain our lives. Nature is filled with examples of gentleness. Let them inspire you. Nature is ceaselessly singing God's glory.

To cultivate the gentleness that is already within, you follow spiritual practices. Take a few minutes now and become aware of the gentle energy coursing through your being. Your entire body is gentle. It is supple, it is soft, it is creative. Your inbreath is gentle; your outbreath is gentle, soft, wonderful, supple, creative, full of love. Your mind is gentle. It has gentle thoughts, noble thoughts, creative thoughts, loving thoughts. Your heart, the temple of God, is gentle. It has gentle feelings, creative feelings; it is full of love, full of energy.

As you breathe in, breathe the gentleness of the universe: the gentle earth, the gentle waters, the gentle flames, the gentle winds, the gentle ether. As you breathe out, let the gentle thoughts, the gentle feelings, the gentle vibrations permeate the universe. Offer gentleness to the universe. In turn, let the universe offer gentleness to you. By receiving your gentleness, the universe becomes strong. By accepting gentleness from the universe, you become strong. Your conviction, your determination, your perseverance and commitment — all are augmented by gentleness.

Let your whole body relax. Let your mind become more serene. Let your heart expand. Experience gentleness in your own being, and carry this awareness as you walk through your days. Remember a gentle word or thought or feeling; or a gentle smile or look; or something that reminds you of gentleness in nature, in people, in situations, in books you have read. Allow gentleness to permeate your consciousness. Even if other thoughts come, don't worry. You need not reject this thought or that thought, thinking "This is good" and "That is not good." You don't have to push your thoughts away; you can transform them into gentleness. You can embrace all your thoughts. You can be filled with enthusiasm and sing God's glory.

With great respect, with great love, I welcome you all with all my heart.

*Sadgurunāth mahārāj kī jay!*

Chapter 11

# Untangling the Mesh of Envy

With great respect, with great love, I welcome you all with all my heart.

To be enthusiastic in the real sense of the word is to feel lighthearted — and this is the philosophy of Siddha Yoga: to experience the scintillating blue light in every person and object we see; to understand the needs of others; to feel the gentle, loving, and secure pulse of the heart at all times; to be able to walk lightly and speak sweetly; to be able to sing God's glory without limitation; to see all creatures as one great family of God; to recognize the supreme Self in everything and everyone — this is our goal. This is our intention. This is our path.

It is a supreme undertaking. To fulfill it, your heart must be pure, your mind must be peaceful, your actions must be focused, your way of life must be clean and guided by higher principles. For this, you do sadhana, spiritual practices. Meditation, self-inquiry, chanting, selfless service, study of the scriptures, austerity — these and many other practices are valuable means of purifying the mind and the heart.

Baba Muktananda used to say, "Take a broom and sweep your heart." What happens inside when you hear this message of Baba's? Doesn't it stir a resolve to rise to the challenge? The *shakti* that Baba puts into every word makes his command so appealing. You feel his support in every bit of effort you make to clear away each obstacle. All you have to do is — just do it. And you are determined. You keep the mind and the heart clean so they can reflect the light of God. This is a great *dhāranā* to practice: "I want to reflect God's light. I want to sing God's glory." However, in the course of the day, in the midst of an action, one often forgets.

When this happens, when the sublime teachings of the great ones and the miraculous effects of spiritual practice fall to one side, then what takes place? Something begins to corrode the priceless power of the mind. Something veils the light of the heart, the sweetest temple of God. A person no longer has access to the nectar of his or her own heart. Something begins to eat away at the roots of enthusiasm and stifle the ability to sing God's glory. What is it that pulls a seeker away from the luminosity in this divine world? Examine your own heart a bit. What is it that takes you away from the Truth, from the light of God? What is it that shrouds the temple of God? If it is not anger, laziness, ambition, or greed, if it is not pride at this moment, what could it be that takes you away from God?

All the knowers of the Truth — the saints and great ones, the philosophers, the great seekers, monks and ascetics, enlightened beings — all who wrote commentaries on spiritual texts, and truly speaking, all who understand the nature of the mind say the same thing: it is envy. Hundreds of stories and fables and anecdotes graphically describe envy and the results it produces. Envy ruins people's lives. Thousands of songs lament the endless woes created by envy. Millions of incidents have been recorded with the details of all the misery that envy brings into your life.

Think of the *Mahābhārata*. Everyone's ruin is due to envy: envious Duryodhana, envious Shakuni. Think of the *Rāmāyana*. The sole reason the *Rāmāyana* epic took place was because Manthara, who was envious, went to one of the queens and filled her ears with envy, and therefore, Lord Rama was banished into the forest for fourteen years. Practically any tragic story is based on envy. So it's not as if anyone is blind to this problem. It's not as if anyone is immune to envy, either. Envy is malicious. Think of the damage it does, both to the one who envies and to the one who is the object of envy. Even though this is well known, nonetheless, it is so easy to fall prey to this deadly inner enemy. Why? Have you asked yourself why you succumb so easily to this thief of the heart?

There is a certain rush of pleasure that goes with envy. All living beings, and particularly human beings, like the rush of pleasure. And for this thrill of pleasure, one will do almost anything. Like the rush of desire, the excitement of envy can be very seductive. You feel somehow enlivened by the heat of its movement. Though what you feel for someone you envy cannot precisely be called love, it has all the energy of attraction. There is such attraction in being envious: attraction to another's advantages, possessions, privileges, relationships, talents, attainments. You are continually looking at the other person. Do you wish you were that person? No. You just want what they have.

Envy arises like pleasure, but in no time at all, you are caught in its whirlpool. And then it is like drowning in poison. Isn't this what envy does? Envy turns sweetness to acid and enthusiasm into spite. It is the opposite of compassion. Envy is the close friend of the other villains that plot in the dark corners of the heart: desire, anger, greed, pride, and delusion. These thieves of the heart are so closely interwoven, so interconnected, that when one of them thrives, the others also profit. They are in partnership, and unfortunately, they never dissolve this partnership. Their hands are bound to one another. Can you imagine what an incredible fortress they have built within you?

Think of the situations that tempt you to indulge in envy. You must understand one thing: we are not talking about having just a moment of envy or anger or greed. As you follow the spiritual path, you come to understand it is your desire to *indulge* in these feelings that causes the real problems. Think of situations that have tempted you to indulge in envy, to linger in envy, and how the more envious you became, the more enmeshed you felt. Sometimes when Baba would tell someone that another person was having great meditation experiences, the first person would immediately try to tell Baba what a bad person the "good meditator" really was. Consider your own life and try to see when envy arises within you and how you indulge in it. Think honestly about what makes you envious. When do you experience that terrible acid in your stomach?

Do you ever feel envious when you hear people sharing wonderful meditation experiences?

Do you ever feel envious when your friend seems to have an easier life than you do?

Do you feel envious when someone you know receives a gift you have been coveting for a long time?

When you are full of envy, how can you drink the nectar of the inner Self? How can you find the peace of your quiet mind? How can you be filled with enthusiasm and sing God's glory? A devotee cries out:

> O Lord, O pure One, how can I come to Your door
> wearing this dirty cloak?
> I feel very ashamed.
>
> O Lord, how can I appear before You
> wearing this dirty cloak?
> You have given me such a pure body,
> such a clean mind.
> I feel so ashamed.
>
> I have spent all my time in sense pleasures alone.
> I have gotten so entangled in this world.
> I have used this pure body to indulge
> in the impure things of this world.
> The stains on my cloak are one too many,
> lifetime after lifetime.
>
> Even though You have given me a pure body,

I have been wearing this dirty cloak.
How can I remove these stains now?[1]

This is a heartfelt prayer. When you feel this way, you want to become free from *samskāras*, or traces of memory, and from habits that leave you open to vices like envy. But then, you are enmeshed in the thicket of envy. Getting out of it is really very difficult. The scriptures say that one single desire allowed to run rampant gives rise to a dark quality like envy. But what if you catch that one desire before it runs rampant, when it is still in an early stage? Can't you examine its worth then and uproot it if you choose? That is the most difficult part — to catch it and examine it right in the beginning. You think it is pleasurable, you think it feels good, so why try to get rid of it? You must have experienced this in your own life and seen it in the lives of others as well. You know someone is going down the wrong path, and you tell them so. But they argue with you and say, "It doesn't make me feel bad, so why should I stop?" Or they say, "I don't care if it brings about my destruction. Taking the wrong path feels so good."

The Upanishads say that in the beginning pleasures seem to be so wonderful, but remember, in the end they turn into pain.[2] There is so much to let go of if you want to grow. If you let envy go unchecked and unacknowledged, then trying to handle the immensity of its consequences is monumental. If you can recognize the first rumbling of a desire that is going to lead you to envy, then you can clear it out of your heart fairly easily. When you first see dust on a window, you can just fan it with a dry cloth, and the dust will fly away. You can clean the window very well. But if you say, "I'll clean it tomorrow, I'll do it the next day, or the next day, or the day after that," and you let a month or two go by, then it becomes much more difficult. Then you have to hire a cleaning service, and more time and expense are involved. Think of the desires that lead to envy. If you don't clean them up right away, you know what happens — the thicket grows.

The *Vijñāna Bhairava*, one of the texts of Kashmir Shaivism, is a treasure chest of *dhāranās*, centering techniques, for meditation and contemplation. Each *dhāranā* is very strong, allowing the attention to settle down through the layers and layers of thought and distraction, until finally your awareness reaches the still pool in the depths of your consciousness. It is just like meditating. You sit for meditation and your mind wanders, you have many, many thoughts. But you just continue to sit, repeating your mantra, watching your breath, visualizing the *sushumnā nādī*. And after a while you notice your mind is settling down, and then, boom! You are in a state of meditation. *Dhāranās* are just like that. One of the verses of the *Vijñāna Bhairava* says:

> If a seeker roots out a desire as soon as it springs up, it will be absorbed in the place from which it arose.[3]

Each time there is a flutter of desire in the heart or the mind, like leaves trembling on a branch before a storm, ask yourself, "Where does this come from? What is at stake? Do I really want it? Is it good for me? Is it good for others? Is there goodness in this?" Once you are clear about its origin, you can decide whether you want it to continue or whether you want it to dissolve back into its source, which is Consciousness. As you know, desires that are not kept in check swarm like hornets dislodged from their nest, flying around madly stinging everyone and everything within reach. Of course, this rooting out has to be a continuous practice. You can't say, "Every Monday I'm going to uproot my envy." It doesn't work like that. The way to gain control over your desires is to look at them face-to-face, day after day, without being ashamed of them; to have the courage to look at what you feel, to look at what's coming up for you; and then to deal with it immediately.

Desires are part of you. If your finger becomes slightly infected, you don't cut it off and throw it away. In the same way, you don't have to be ashamed of your desires. Let a desire come up, look at it, talk to it, and decide whether you want to keep it or whether you want to say, "Goodbye. You are not for me, and I am not for you. We are not meant for each other."

Eventually, you can get to the point where no desire will take on a life of its own unless you give it your permission. This does take practice.

If you are not in control of your desires, they will end up controlling you. If dark impulses such as envy gain a foothold as a result of desires, they will strangle you subtly. You won't even know they are there. All you know is that you seem to be under some kind of spell. Something is happening, but you don't know what. You feel as if you are somehow intoxicated. This is the trickiest aspect of these six enemies. When you are experiencing them, you feel a kind of "high," and that's what is very deceiving. Because you think you are feeling so good, you believe that whatever is happening must be good for you. Envy often feels like a kind of intoxication that you think everyone else should also enjoy. For example, some people see others who are extremely happy on their spiritual path. They become envious of them and they say, "Why are these people following the spiritual path? They should be living a worldy life; they should be doing what we're doing." And they try to destroy the happiness of others. What's really happening is that they are being deluded, blinded by envy. But sooner or later, one way or another, envy does you in. It has always been so.

How do you combat envy? How do you develop the ability to seize hold of a desire that is still in seed form? In a talk many years ago to seekers in Gurudev Siddha Peeth, Baba gave a beautiful answer to this:

> You should always contemplate these things: Why was I born? Why do I follow the spiritual path? After living in the ashram, what have I attained? After chanting so much, after doing so many *Guru Gītās*, how much have I been transformed from within? Your heart can bear testimony to this.

Contemplation and self-inquiry are so valuable. You really need to understand why you are on the spiritual path, why you follow the practices and come to the ashram. It is very good to put Baba's contemplation into practice: "Why was I born? Why do I follow spiritual practices? After coming to the ashram, what have I attained?"

Listen carefully to what Baba said next:

> If even a spark of love arises in your heart, then your life is changed. You come to the spiritual path for this love, this love that changes your life completely. Your desires turn into desirelessness. Anger turns into love. Hostility turns into universal brotherhood. How much universal brotherhood do you feel for others? How much love do you have? Look at it yourself. How do you behave? Try to find out how much freer you have become from hatred and jealousy.

These contemplations are truly a great cleansing process. They bring everything back to its source, back into focus. They make you re-evaluate your intentions. They are like a magnifying glass that you place over your mind and your heart. Then you can see what has been collecting inside the pure temple of God in your heart and inside your priceless mind.

When you deprive yourself of this profound contemplation, your mind and heart become crammed with negative thoughts. This actually creates a kind of reverse cycle of energy — like when a film is run backward and water appears to flow upward. Just think of how it makes you feel when you see something as unnatural as this. It almost makes your stomach queasy. Think of a clock running backward, or the counterclockwise movement of something that is supposed to go in a clockwise direction. Aren't they reversing the cycle of energy? When the body gets sick, it is due to the reverse cycle of energy. Have you noticed? Sometimes you see a friend, and there is something about the person that makes you uneasy. You can't put your finger on it; you can't really tell what it is. However, within a short time you find out that the person is suffering from a serious disease, and that is what you were picking up.

When there is a reverse cycle of energy, you are immediately aware that something is wrong, but you don't always know what it is. Sometimes people's energy is completely toxic. It may be because of the food they eat or the thoughts they have. Food and thoughts are closely interrelated. A reverse cycle of energy is created if the food you eat and the thoughts you have are not conducive to your health, if they are not pure. This reverse cycle of energy is created by envy as well.

Your inner being is the home of divine feelings. They are meant to nurture you. They are food for your soul. They make the mind and the heart beat to the pulse of oneness with God. They bring you the experience that everything is God's. They make you aware that life itself is a marvelous creation of God. You understand that this universe is God's body, and you are following God's will.

Why, if everything is God's, do you envy others? As everyone knows, the simple truth is that you feel incomplete, deprived, and it seems to you that what someone else has is the answer to your lack. You feel lonely, and so you feel envious of others. All that is projection, of course, and you know it. But the important thing to notice is that envy blocks you at the level of "have" and "have not." "I have this, and I don't have that. He has this, and he doesn't have that." Envy enacts a drama of wants and desires — a great Broadway show goes on inside you.

All human beings are naturally attracted to things that are beautiful, loving, sweet, kind, generous, and selfless. This is the natural flow of the heart. If people are sweet and kind, immediately you want to be in their company. It is human nature to long for the shining virtues — knowledge, forgiveness, patience. People seek what is lofty, Godlike, and spiritually full. At the same time, they harbor envy. And not only that, they behave as if envy were a natural, justified reaction. Isn't it amazing? They say, "Ah! What can I do? That person makes me envious." They think that's what they are entitled to feel. It's so strange. The heart should be bathing in the nectar of contentment, but instead it burns in the fire of envy. And it doesn't matter how many possessions people have. The more they have, often the more envy they feel. Do they ever think of getting rid of their envy? Many people say they are still processing their envy. What that usually means is they want to keep on indulging it, and they talk about their process for hours on end.

These people do want to let go — but not right now, not this instant. They still want a chance to project their negative thoughts onto another person so that the other person won't flourish. They want just a little more time and then, perhaps, they will think of taking a shower so they can purify themselves.

It is such an irony, isn't it? People have so little control over their emotions. Even though they are God-loving, philanthropic seekers of the Truth, they constantly glorify envy and let it destroy their goodness.

Always be vigilant. Otherwise, before you know it, envy will take up all the space in your heart. It tends to do that. Even though your heart is meant to sing God's name, envy seeps into all the domains of your life, and you rarely discover it until it's too late. Suddenly, you realize the wellspring of enthusiasm has dried up, and your heart refuses to sing God's glory. Whenever you say you have no more interest in spiritual practices, look into your heart and try to see what thoughts you have been having and what actions you have been performing. I want you to know, the wellspring of spiritual practices never dries up. The more spiritual practices you do with the right attitude, the more experiences you will have, and the greater these experiences will be. Spiritual practices are never to be blamed. They are beyond reproach. What you need to look at is your own mind.

Once there was a wily old maid who never performed any good actions. Even though she was fortunate in her work and served a very rich merchant, she spent all her time burning in envy. When she cooked, she burned with envy. When she swept the floors, she burned with envy. When she spoke to the neighbors, it was the same. If the merchant spoke to a beautiful woman, the old maid burned in envy. Even though she was old, still she would burn. If the merchant brought home wonderful guests, she would burn with envy, seeing their happiness and their goodness. She spent more energy on envy than she did on her household duties.

One day a beggar came to the door and in the sweetest way requested her help. "Will you please give me something to eat? I am really hungry. For the sake of God?" Now she had never done any charitable work, but her heart stirred, just a little. Maybe it was her good fortune. She went to the kitchen and looked in the pantry for the smallest, driest little carrot. She gave it to him, telling him what a great charity she was performing.

He was very happy with the carrot because he was so hungry. He offered his thanks and blessings, and left. After some time, it happened — as it happens to everyone — that the old maid died. The messenger of death came to take her soul away. She had to pass through the Department of Karma, where they checked her Karma Book. Much to their amazement, they saw that she was one of those rare people who had not performed a single good action. But then, a shining little blue dot appeared, so they looked again, and they found that she had performed one little good action. She had once given a tiny, dry carrot to a hungry beggar.

The officials explained, "Your karmas are pretty bad so you'll have to spend a thousand years in hell. Nevertheless, this one good action you performed will give you a glimpse of heaven. Which would you like to do first — have the darshan of heaven? Or spend a thousand years in hell?"

She said, "I want to have the darshan of heaven first."

"Fine," they said. And immediately, a beautiful, long, luminous carrot appeared. It was very, very big. They told her, "Hold on to it. It will take you to heaven."

Without wasting a second, she grabbed the carrot. She embraced it with all her might. And the carrot began to ascend toward heaven. Now there were many many other souls also waiting there for judgment, and when they saw the carrot moving upward, carrying the old maid, they thought, "That's the darshan line going to heaven!" Right away, someone grabbed the old maid's feet because he thought in that way he would get to heaven too. And then another person held on to *his* feet. And another and another. They all thought since their Karma Books had not been tallied yet, no one would know about their bad karmas and they would get to stay in heaven forever. The big, luminous orange carrot was going higher and higher, carrying the old maid and all the people. By now there were a hundred people trying to get to heaven.

The old maid looked down and saw all those people holding on to her feet, getting a free ride. She thought, "Wait a minute! This is *my* good karma. What makes them think *they* are going to get there without having worked for it. No way! I have suffered so much in my life." And she got really angry, really envious that these people were going to heaven because of her merit. She tried to get rid of them by knocking them off with both hands. As soon as she let go of the carrot, the old maid and all the other people came tumbling down to earth. And the beautiful, big, luminous carrot kept going higher and higher toward heaven.

So there you have it. That which is good remains good and takes you to heaven. And envy takes you to hell.

Once in a question-and-answer session, someone prefaced a question to Baba by saying, "I am never satisfied with what I have. How can I overcome this?"

Baba replied, "You become dissatisfied with what you have

because you are not aware of all that you have. If you were aware of all that you have, it would give you supreme satisfaction, and the question of being dissatisfied would not arise at all. Everyone suffers from this tendency."

What does Baba mean? What is it that you have? Pure Consciousness, the light of God, perfect peace, and joy without end. You have a beautiful path, great friends, a divine ashram. In Gurudev Siddha Peeth, when we were young, sometimes we would act envious of one another and Baba would say to us, "You have so much. You have this beautiful ashram to stay in. Three times a day food is served to you. You go to the Temple and chant the *Āratī* three times a day. You receive so much energy from Bhagawan Nityananda. You are living in this beautiful place where the sages have done *tapasya* for centuries and centuries, and because of them you don't have to do much *tapasya*. You can just experience the scintillating energy and their *shakti*. You have so much! What are you envious about?"

Such things are the source of supreme satisfaction. Compared to them, it is a trifling thing to envy someone's new car or new job. Think about it — you have so much, knowing that God dwells within you as you.

One of the saints of modern India, Rama Tirtha, says:

> By Your grace, O Lord, one is freed from want.
> Is there anything that cannot be obtained from You?
> But what can I do? My bag is so small. My heart is so tiny.
> I can't even take everything that You want to give me.
>
> What does it matter if God looks at you,
> or away from you?
> If you experience this separation, it cannot be called love.
> O Lord, only by Your grace can I be free from this envy,
> from want.
> There's nothing You don't want to give me.
> But what can I do? My heart is so small.
> It cannot take everything You want to give.[4]

The supreme understanding of contentment is what will take you across. God holds nothing back. Like the sun, God gives abundantly because giving is His nature. He can't do anything but give. He will always give. God makes no judgment about who gets what. Depending on the size of your bag, depending on your own worthiness, you receive and maintain the gifts of grace. You allow them to grow. Your own capacity is the only frontier you have. Baba's advice is so beautiful. He tells us to be continually conscious of the ripples of the mind and the vibrations of the heart. Just as a sailor uses a compass to check his direction and steer his ship, you use the meter of contemplation to take the temperature of your own mind and monitor its tendencies. If you do this in an honest and righteous way, unfailingly you will come to see God's bounty, God's generosity. The only limitation is how much you are willing to apply yourself to the Truth.

The cure for envy is contentment, supreme contentment. From your own experience, you will come to see that contentment is the antidote to all the inner enemies, such as anger and greed. If you have contentment, then you have mastery over the six inner enemies. Of course, contentment is a very high state, not something you can talk your mind into. It is an experience you cultivate, a state you attain. You learn to be full and satisfied no matter what happens, no matter how much or how little you receive. To have the divine company of contentment, you have to be very fortunate. Contentment does not mean complacency. Contentment is the power to accept whatever comes your way and add it to the fullness within.

The Sufi Master Sheikh Sa'di says, "He that envies is possessed of self-made hurts." The envy that you court spins a tapestry of hurtfulness from within. It presents you with a distorted picture of the world. And once you see the world in this way, you realize that all the wounds you incur are self-inflicted. No one else is cutting your lifeline. No one else has the power to do that. If you can remember this, then perhaps you will be able to let go of envy and be attracted instead by the light of the inner flame.

There is another aspect of envy that must be mentioned before we finish, and that is how envy looks for company. People who are well-versed in the ways of envy are also quite expert at exciting envy in others. You really need to think about this — how you create envy in others. It is the nature of all living beings to look for their own clan — even viruses want to multiply — and in the same way, envy wants to see itself everywhere. It doesn't like to survive all by itself. Envy really likes company.

The way you can continue to be enthusiastic and sing God's glory is by eliminating the effects of envy, continually taking the temperature of your mind and heart, and not allowing envy to eat up the light of your own goodness. When envy does arise, look at it and see how best you can uproot it. That's the only way you can maintain your enthusiasm and sing God's glory; otherwise, you'll just be looking at others and depriving yourself of spiritual experiences. And you'll be singing the glory of envy, not the glory of God.

For a few moments right now, contemplate how you have participated in spreading the disease of envy. Perhaps you have acted like you are part of some important inner circle. You have acted "in the know" about "secret things." You have been careful to make sure the people around you understand that you know something very important that they don't know, so they will feel envious of you. Or, if you are feeling envious because you are not part of some "special" group, do you make sure your friends also know that they have missed out on something? Or do you leave them in peace? Think about this: How has envy spread to you? How have you spread envy? Through one action or another, through one word or another, through one piece of behavior or another, how have you affected your world with envy? What has it done to your mind and heart? How has it kept you away from your spiritual practices? How has it made you throw away your spiritual values?

Just for a few moments become aware of all the wonderful things you have in your life. Even the tiniest bit of good fortune is worthy of acknowledgment. Become aware of all the great blessings in your life. As the breath comes in and the breath goes out, allow your mind to become content with everything you have and everything you don't have. The mind is content. The heart is content. Your whole being is suffused with contentment.

The absence of envy, *vimatsara*, will enable you to experience your own enthusiasm and sing God's glory. It is a good thing to practice contemplating your state every night before you go to bed. Even if you haven't had a chance to do it throughout the day, check to see how lighthearted you are when you go to bed. How much enthusiasm have you evoked in others? How much of God's glory have you been able to experience and share? How much of God's glory have you been able to spread? That's what you want to spread — God's glory, not envy.

Baba once said: "It is our foremost duty to spread the awareness of universal brotherhood everywhere. We should spread it in our neighborhood, in our country, and in every place we go. Today we do not need to worry about success and failure. We do not need to burn in the pride of superiority or inferiority. Instead, we need to experience the love that comes from having an awareness of universal brotherhood. We need to practice having affection for other people all the time."

This is the ultimate state, the absence of envy, *vimatsara*. When you are free of envy, entirely free, you are filled with enthusiasm and you sing God's glory.

With great respect, with great love, I welcome you all with all my heart.

*Sadgurunāth mahārāj kī jay!*

*Chapter 12*

# Seva Creates a Pond of Nectar

With great respect, with great love, I welcome you all with all my heart.

Many of you have spent time in Shree Muktananda Ashram and participated in the practices of the *gurukula.* Do you remember the first time you came to the ashram? For some of you perhaps it was twenty years ago, for some eleven years ago, and some of you may have entered the ashram for the first time quite recently. Do you remember what happened when you first stepped into the ashram, when you walked on the ashram grounds? The very first time you walked through the gate, what impressed you the most? What was the first hint, the first clue, that this was not an ordinary place?

Some people marvel at the gardens. Others marvel at its cleanliness. They marvel at the glow on people's faces. They marvel at a feeling of something scintillating in the air: "There's something in the air. I don't know what it is." They feel gentle, forceful energy brush over them. Perhaps they have heard of the *shakti,* perhaps they have not. It doesn't really matter. People are affected by the serene beauty of the ashram atmosphere. They are touched by the love that shimmers undeniably in every particle of the ashram. Some people are believers when they come; others are skeptics; yet others are full of negativities. That doesn't really matter either. Somehow their hearts are stirred.

People who come to the ashram do experience something

wonderful, powerful, and profound. They cannot always define it, yet it is the first intimation that this is a sacred place. What grips the heart so positively, so unmistakably? What is it that captivates each one's heart? What is the undeniable force that underlies the beauty of the gardens? What is the practice that sustains the unfolding of the *shakti*?

It is seva, selfless service. Seva, the most wonderful, the most powerful, and the most profound alchemy. It is work performed without attachment; duty fulfilled without any desire for personal gain; service offered without any motive, without any of the objectives that cramp one's actions or contract the heart. Seva means giving one's time and energy without any strings attached and therefore being able to work with total freedom. Seva means doing work for the sake of the highest purpose, doing work while you recognize the worth of another human being, and keeping the value of life in mind. Seva means doing work as a form of worship, a way of singing God's glory, an offering for the sake of supreme love. Seva is doing work in such a way that it is grace in action, devotion in action, knowledge in action.

It is truly seva that captures people's fascination when they enter the ashram. Seva reveals the glory of the heart. This mysterious practice can be measured in hours but not in its effect on the heart — its visible and invisible blessings. Seva is built into every brick of the ashram and sings through every petal of every flower. It is seva that accelerates the sadhana of a seeker and lights the path to God. It is seva that removes all the blocks on the spiritual path and supports a seeker all the way to his goal. It is seva that embodies the Guru's love for the disciples. Seva is the most wonderful, the most powerful, the most profound alchemy. You do seva, and you are a changed person — guaranteed for sure.

When you see the ashram, what do you truly perceive? Do you perceive it only with your physical eyes? Blessings have been cultivated here by hours and seasons and years of seva. All this seva has created a pond of nectar where seekers can quench their spiritual thirst. Seva creates a pond of nectar through which you experience the deeper purpose of life, the immortality of the Self.

In the *Bhakti Sūtras*, the celestial sage Narada offers his extraordinary understanding of divine love. This work itself is also an act of selfless service — imparting wisdom to others. According to Narada, one of the principal means of gaining access to divine love is "by uninterrupted, devoted worship,"[1] and this devoted worship is called true service. In the same way, true service is also called devoted worship. In true service, you offer your seva to the Lord and you feel one with Him. You offer your seva to a place and you are bonded with that place. If you don't feel comfortable in a place, offer your work, and you will see — immediately a bond is created.

Divine love is attained by the continual offering of worship in action, which is service that is free from motives. Divine love is sustained in the same way. To be really enthusiastic and sing God's glory, your seva must be prolonged and ardent. Until you give yourself to the highest and greatest purpose, until you truly apply yourself to something very meaningful, it is difficult to experience your own inner goodness. And it is practically impossible to appreciate all the things you are constantly receiving from God.

It is something of a paradox that to understand what you have received, you have to give. There is no way around it. Giving is what opens your eyes — the inner eye, the eye of wisdom. Learning to give and having the willingness and good karma to receive — that is the greatest gift of seva. The willingness to give and receive is a boon. This is true not only in the ashram or on the spiritual path but in worldly life as well. The world functions smoothly and very beautifully when most of the work is done not for money, but as an offering of one's virtues, kindness, and generosity. The world flourishes when people are able to support one another, keeping money out of the picture; when they can support one another emotionally and spiritually; when they can genuinely be there for one another, offering service.

Anyone who has become truly great must have offered loving service in an uninterrupted fashion. For different people, it takes different forms. Some people may have the good fortune to work for the needy. Others may toil in the field and feed people through their labor. Some people may have the good fortune to serve great beings, and others to impart wisdom to students, helping to form young minds. Some people may have the good fortune to stay up all night and guarantee the peace in which others sleep. Others may have the great fortune of praying for the upliftment of their fellow human beings and for the world. That may be their seva: to pray all the time for others, for their brothers and sisters, for universal brotherhood, universal sisterhood. Some people may have the great good fortune to make it possible for others to attend satsang, to chant, and to meditate.

What is important in seva are certain invariable criteria that reveal the depth of your offering. These criteria are, first, the attitude with which you offer your service; second, the intention behind your service; third, your expectation of reward; fourth, your willingness to offer your service; and fifth, the way you perform your seva. For example, how careful are you of other people? Are you sensitive to others? How mindfully are your actions performed? How much do you truly give, and how much do you hold back? How constant are your efforts? All this matters greatly. As long as your seva is free from attachment and selfish motives, it will bear the highest fruit.

However, as soon as the tiniest twinge of greed, the smallest flicker of pride, or the most microscopic stab of envy enters the arena of seva, then everything becomes quite muddled. You get so embroiled in *māyā*, illusion, that you don't understand what is going on. You are not able to separate the effects of the mind from the fruit of seva. In fact, you may be completely confused even as you are being thrashed to the ground again and again by the blows of your own inner enemies. Most frequently, you will blame it all on the world outside: "That person makes me so mad." "Aren't Mondays always a drag?" "No one really understands my values." "I am not really cut out for this kind of seva."

But almost without exception, the root of the problem is inside. It takes a mountain of your own good-naturedness to lift you above these complaints that pollute the awareness of seva. Seva itself is utterly pure, utterly pristine, and mysteriously purifying. Seva is a spiritual practice. It is not a one-time undertaking or a punishment or an obligation. It is really not an obligation.

Sometimes you hear about people who have committed some crime, but rather than going to prison, they are given the chance to do, say, five hundred hours of community service. Now, let's be very clear. The seva, selfless service, that we are talking about is not a punishment or a sentence or a form of parole. Don't let these ideas get confused. However, when a person offers community service, it *is* a way of purifying himself. Perhaps in ancient times, this practice did arise from a true understanding, from great wisdom. Instead of worrying all his life about the crime he committed or the blunder he made, a person actually offered his service. In this way he cleansed himself and became free from the stains of guilt. When they created the system of a certain number of hours of community service to relieve a person of a crime, I do believe that they were thinking about purifying the mind, the heart, the very being, and in this way, re-establishing a person's self-respect, as well as the respect of the community and the world. It was a way of regaining the understanding that one was a good citizen of this world after all.

As you apply yourself to the beautiful and rewarding practice of seva, your age-old impurities are cleared away. Inner knowledge begins to sprout with fresh blossoms of understanding. You feel fresh energy moving through your being. Haven't you experienced this?

You are doing seva, and all of a sudden an incredible puzzle, something that was giving you a headache, is solved.

Or you have a brilliant idea, and with this idea you make greater progress on the spiritual path.

Or suddenly you are offered a great job.

Or you become a better friend of someone whom you have been wanting to know for a long time.

Or all of a sudden the inner doors open and light comes flooding in, and you bathe in this incredible inspiration, this enthusiasm, and you sing God's glory — all because of seva.

As you continue to do selfless service, your surrender to seva becomes deeper and deeper. You want to do seva not because you have to, but because it creates a pond of nectar, a river of love. You become the recipient of this beautiful gift, and others too experience great sweetness and divinity. They are able to see the reflection of God in your seva. It is almost as though when you do seva you are handing God to someone. You are holding God in your arms and saying to others, "Come and share in the glory of God. Come and experience the glory of God." When you do seva, you give a true form to God, a form you can see and hear and be with. Rather than experiencing terrible loneliness, you live constantly with the embodiment of the Truth. You are touching God. Tukaram Maharaj says that when you repeat God's name He is dancing on your tongue, He is dancing in your heart, you are actually giving birth to God in your own being. And the same is true for seva. You are giving birth to God's love, God's light. You are giving birth to God, to divinity. You are holding God, you are giving God, you are being with God all the time.

There comes a time when you begin to experience an incredible hunger for seva. You want to do more and more seva, not only when you are physically using your hands, but also in a subtle way. You are constantly thinking about how well you can do the work, how best you can give yourself to it, and how you can carry it to other places and share it with others. Through your thoughts you are doing seva. Through your speech you are doing seva. Wherever you go, you are doing seva. You begin to see that seva is truly a unique gift from God. You begin to experience that seva creates a pond of nectar. You begin to know that seva is the most wonderful, the most powerful, the most profound alchemy.

Once there was a Sufi saint named Ibrahim. Before he became a renunciant, he was a king. When he was an old man, he told a story about the early days of his sadhana. Ibrahim recalled, "Once I bought a slave. Since the man was going to become a member of my household, I began to ask him some questions. I said, 'What is your name?'

" 'Whatever you call me,' he answered.

" 'What do you eat?'

" 'Whatever you give me.'

" 'What do you want to wear?'

" 'Whatever you give me to wear.'

" 'What do you want to do?'

" 'Whatever you command.'

" 'What do you truly desire?' I finally asked.

"He replied, 'What does a servant have to do with desire?'

"I said to myself, 'What a wretched man am I. All my life I have thought of myself as a servant of God. Now, let me learn from this man what it means to be a true servant.' And I wept so long that I fainted."

This was a turning point in Ibrahim's sadhana — an awakening to the understanding of selfless service. Such abandonment! Abandonment of what? Selfishness. Complete surrender before God, before the Master. Complete faith that God will provide, protect, and uplift you, no matter what. Actually, a slave who could speak like this was no ordinary man. Such a pristine attitude toward seva is not easy to come by. He had to have been a saint, a great being, a realized soul. Such things do happen;

enlightened beings are found in every walk of life.

Now, don't make the mistake of thinking that this is just a story about a slave and a master. It portrays the perfect understanding of seva. True seva, this story tells us, is a matter of performing one's duty without attachment and without the desires that taint the offering of seva. As Baba Muktananda once said: "A pure servant is not even conscious of the fact that he is putting in selfless service. If he is conscious of it, it means that his heart is still impure. A pure servant has absolutely no craving, no desire."

Guru Nanak, the great mystic and master of the Sikh tradition, had two grown sons. One day he called for his older son, Shri Chand, and said, "I am growing old. It is time for me to put all my affairs in order. Of all that I have to give, tell me, what do you want?"

"Father," replied Shri Chand, "I want the experience of the inner Self and devotion to the Lord. That is all I care about."

"So be it," said Nanak. "You will have your wish." And he sent him on his way.

Then Nanak called for his younger son, Lakshmi Das, and asked him the same question: "What do you want? Ask anything of me and it shall be yours."

The second son answered, "I am not really interested in spiritual things, Father. I want worldly prosperity."

Guru Nanak nodded and assured him that plenty of money, a house, a happy family, and comforts of every kind would be his; and he sent him on his way.

Then Guru Nanak called for one of his disciples who was named Angaddev. He said to him, "Angaddev, what do you want? Ask anything of me, anything you wish."

Without hesitation, Angaddev said, "What could I want? You have given me everything that I should have. O Gurudev, if you must give me something, give me the grace to serve you. I am not interested in realization or liberation. All I want to do is serve you forever."

That very day Guru Nanak made his decision. He named Angaddev his successor.

Angaddev had attained the high state of desirelessness: wanting nothing, craving nothing, yearning for nothing. This state has immense power. When you want nothing, the Lord gives you everything. When you go after things, they run away from you. When you do seva, you are laying the foundation of this beautiful state. It is a tremendous task to sustain desirelessness as you perform all your actions. Yet all along the way, even as seva purifies you, it gives you glimpses of its sublime sweetness and profundity.

The ancient *Rig Veda* says:

> The one who dedicates his life to the service of the Lord, whom the Lord takes into His loving fold, finds himself twice blessed by the supreme celestial powers. He basks happily in the sunshine of God's love.[2]

Seva creates a pond of nectar. People who have understood the significance of seva yearn to taste its nectar. They actually feel quite dejected if the opportunity passes them by. They feel the loss acutely because they know that the chance to do seva is a matter of tremendous fortune. In fact, second best to *shaktipāt* is seva. Truly, you have to be very fortunate to be able to serve. It is your own worthiness that gives you the power to offer God to other people. You are bringing God to life. Anyone who misses the opportunity to do seva feels dejected. Anyone who knows the importance of seva really weeps, saying, "I am not doing enough seva."

Janabai, one of the great poet-saints of Maharashtra, was a householder and had to work very hard to keep everyone in the family happy. Yet the whole time, her mind and heart were fixed on the Lord. There was never a doubt about whom she was really serving with every one of her actions. Her devotion was so great, so splendid, that the Lord Himself came and regularly worked alongside her. Can you imagine such a thing? You are working and doing seva — and next to you is God. Next to you is Krishna or Shiva or Ganesha. Next to you is Lakshmi, Saraswati, or Durga. Next to you is your chosen Beloved, supporting you all along the way. Yet Janabai's humility never developed a crust of pride; she felt she could never do enough seva. In one of her *abhangas*, Janabai poured out her heart saying:

O Lord, I have done no seva.
    My heart feels such pain.
My heart is aching. What can I do?
I have done no seva.
I am a sinner after all.
I have hardly meditated on You.
I have done no seva.

O Lord, will You tell me what I should do?
I have done no seva.
    I have not given myself to You.
I feel that I have destroyed my life.
I haven't even meditated on You properly.
Yet whenever I was in trouble,
    in great pain, You came to my aid.
You are always right beside me.
You underwent torture for my sake.
Day in and day out,
    You helped me grind wheat.
O Lord, I beseech You to forgive me.
Please forgive me for not serving You properly.
Jani, the servant of Namdev,
    offers You her salutations.
O Lord, I have never done enough seva.[3]

The whole world weeps, you know. The whole world suffers. Most of the time, all this weeping is aimless, pointless, unnecessary, and empty. It is useless, senseless, and worthless; fruitless, barren, hollow, sterile, and utterly futile. The long and the short of it is that most people weep when their desires are not met. However, Janabai's weeping was a response to not having the chance to serve God as fully as she wanted to. This kind of weeping opens new doors. When your tears are an expression of your deep yearning to offer yourself in service, they create a path of light. When suffering becomes unbearable because you don't have the time to offer your seva, to give yourself, then know that God is calling you. You are hearing the voice of God. You are feeling the touch of God. When you suffer because the great Lord has not received your seva, it cleanses your heart. This kind of suffering washes away all your impurities. This kind of suffering is divine indeed. In this state, the heart is enfolded by God's tender love.

This is what you hear in Janabai's *abhanga*. From her life story it is very clear she worked selflessly, tirelessly, without ever caring for her own needs. If you read her life story, you will weep from beginning to end, and from then on. She lived such an unbearable life. Yet in her heart, no matter how much seva she did, she felt it was insufficient. How can this be? What did she expect of herself? What did she really want? There is only one answer. She longed to serve so totally there would not be any room left for a single breath that was not drawn for God. She wanted every breath of her being to be at the service of the Lord, every inhalation and exhalation. Janabai was aiming for absolute union with the Lord through the divine practice of seva. She wanted to merge with God through her seva. This is the attitude that the saints have toward service.

Jnaneshwar Maharaj, a great yogi and a sublime poet, wrote a magnificent passage in which he described how he wished to become everything for his Guru. He wanted to be the earth that supported the Guru's feet and the bed upon which the Guru slept.

He wanted to be the water the Guru drank, the clothes the Guru wore, and the fire that warmed the Guru. He even wanted to be in the smiles that people gave to his Guru. At the end of this immensely beautiful passage, Jnaneshwar Maharaj said: "In this way, becoming everything in the world, I will surround my Guru with every conceivable form of service. As long as my body lasts, I will serve him in this way; and after death I will still long to do so."[4]

Baba Muktananda once said:

> If you do the ashram work without any selfish motive, then you will gather enormous *shakti* within you, regardless of the nature of the work you are doing. It is only an unintelligent person who distinguishes between different kinds of ashram work. To an intelligent person who has the right sort of understanding, all forms of work are equally valuable, because they are all service to the Guru.
>
> One who performs worship inside the Temple is doing ashram seva. One who keeps watch of the gate is doing ashram seva, and one who sweeps the floors is doing ashram seva. It is only unintelligent people who think in terms of superior and inferior kinds of work. To the true *bhaktā*, to a true lover of the Guru, it is all *gurusevā*, whether he is keeping watch or performing worship or writing or sweeping.

Baba emphasized this all the time. All sevas are equal. All sevas are praiseworthy. All sevas bear fruit. All sevas are spiritual practices. Baba made seva a pond of nectar. He made seva appear so interesting, wonderful, powerful, and profound. It is truly his grace that sustains us in this awareness of selfless service. Baba's enthusiasm for seva was so great. He gave himself to everything fully. He never held anything back. And to this day, the pond of nectar he created grows bigger and bigger by his grace and by everyone's willingness to serve.

Transcend the worldly barriers of position, authority, name, and fame, and you will find out what seva means. When you do this, you are actually building the merit to enter the palace of your own heart, the kingdom of God. If you refuse to overcome your limitations, then it is very easy to get caught up in the pettiness of this world, even in the ashram, and totally lose sight of what seva is all about. Then it is like trying to clean a dirty mirror with a dirty rag. It doesn't matter how many years you spend cleaning, the dirt will just travel back and forth between the mirror and the rag. Nothing will get clean. The reflection will always be muddy. Perception will be distorted.

Seva cannot be done only with your hands or only with the force of your intellect. Your inner state and your understanding are constantly put to the test. Over and over again, you must remember the five invariable criteria that reveal the depth of your offering of selfless service, divine seva. First, you must scrutinize the attitude with which you offer your seva. Second, you must be very honest: what is the intention behind your seva? Third, what are your expectations for the fruit of your service? Fourth, how willing are you to offer your service without reward? And fifth, you must take a close look at the way you go about performing your service. Ask these five questions of yourself again and again. Answer them truthfully again and again. And like a navigator steering a ship by the stars, you can adjust your position and set your sails so the wind is behind you. You have no idea how much progress you can make when your whole being is aligned with your highest aspiration.

Let your seva be offered with a pure heart. The pure heart scintillates with glorious virtues. Of course, to be able to put these virtues into action requires great inner strength. This is the same strength that enables you to perform your duty without attachment, and this is the key to success. With this inner strength you experience that seva is the most wonderful, the most powerful, and the most profound alchemy ever.

There was once a rabbi who was famous for his holiness and his wisdom. When he was young, he had four assistants. When he grew older, he decided to have only one. People asked him, "Why is it now you have only one helper, one disciple, when previously you had four?"

He said, "Well, I am an old man now, and I cannot serve four disciples."

This anecdote calls for very deep contemplation. In the name of serving, of offering your selfless service, are you the one being served? In the name of being helpful to others, are you the one being helped? In the name of being kind to others, are you living off other people's kindness? In the name of being loving to others, are you becoming a burden? Of course, on the very highest level, you cannot give without receiving — that is the divine law of nature; it is impossible. And also you cannot receive without giving. Absolutely not. Nonetheless, who is working for whom? It is really something to ponder. Who is serving whom?

The one you serve is inside — your God. If you want your seva to bear the sweetest fruit, then you must have the fortitude to contemplate your state of mind. You cannot just clean the mirror. You have to clean the rag as well. You cannot leave yourself out of the equation. A king's treasury must be guarded by all means, or the value of the currency in his kingdom is at risk. In the same way, your hard-earned understanding of the divine nature of seva must be protected by all means if you want to continue on the golden path. Always remember, true seva creates a pond of nectar.

One of the loftiest descriptions of seva is given by Hanuman in the *Rāmāyana*. This great servant of Lord Rama speaks with intimate knowledge and understanding of the practice of selfless service, saying:

> This is my firm conviction. From the point of view of the body, you are the Master and I am the servant. From the

point of view of the embodied soul, you are the Lord and I am your devotee. From the point of view of the supreme Self, you and I are one.[5]

Take a few minutes now and quietly contemplate seva — what you have offered and what you have received. The entire universe is at your service. The earth serves you uninterruptedly. Water serves you uninterruptedly. Fire serves you uninterruptedly. Wind serves you uninterruptedly. The ether serves you uninterruptedly. Because of so many people's selfless service, so many people's kindness, you are able to exist in this universe. You have been given support of every kind — emotional, spiritual, financial — and all this has sustained your life. You cannot exist in this world without other people's service. The birds and animals, the trees and plants — everything in this universe supports you through seva, selfless service. You are given as much as you can receive, as much as you can embrace, as much as you are willing to hold.

Similarly, you cannot exist without offering your service. You have a need to serve. Without serving, you cannot breathe peacefully. When you serve, you are lighthearted. When you do something good for someone else, you are able to sing God's glory. When you say something sweet to someone, when you help someone go to school, when you pull someone out of a ditch, when you show a path to someone, when you sit at the side of someone who is suffering, when you do these kinds of selfless actions without expectation of reward, your heart feels gentle and you sing God's glory. With each inhalation and exhalation, serve the Lord. Offer your selfless service.

You can actually perform everything in your life as seva, whether it is your schoolwork or taking care of a child or doing the budget for the entire nation. If you really look at your work as seva and do it with the highest purpose in mind, then it is a paradise.

Seva creates a pond of nectar. Allow yourself to submerge and emerge, submerge and emerge from this pond of nectar. Allow your entire being to shimmer with the consciousness of seva. Seva is the most powerful, the most wonderful, the most profound alchemy. Contemplate the practice of seva with this awareness: I am here to serve.

With great respect, with great love, I welcome you all with all my heart.

*Sadgurunāth mahārāj kī jay!*

*Chapter 13*

# Gratitude, the Gift of Remembrance

With great respect, with great love, I welcome you all with all my heart.

We have been exploring the different virtues that enable you to experience enthusiasm and give you the power to perceive God's glory everywhere. We have also been looking at some of the less pleasant qualities that tend to prevent you from experiencing enthusiasm. Truly speaking, many of you have not only been looking at these questionable attributes, but you have been making great attempts to renounce them also. This is the greatest form of renunciation: letting go of limiting tendencies so that you can experience your innate enthusiasm and fulfill the beautiful desire to sing God's glory, to see His beauty everywhere.

One of the natural attributes that enables a person to experience enthusiasm is gratitude. Blessed are those who have the heart to appreciate God's bounty. Blessed are those who have encouraged others to praise the Lord. Blessed are those who find deep consolation in the feeling of gratitude. Gratitude occupies a very important place in the lives of seekers. It is a natural response to the Guru's grace, which lifts us out of the dark ages of our ignorance and brings us into the blissful light of God. The Guru's grace puts an end to the suffering of lifetimes and leads us to discover the spontaneous joy that is natural to the heart. The Guru's grace takes away the pettiness of the mind and imparts the sublime wisdom of the Siddhas. By giving *shaktipāt*, divine initiation, the Guru begins the process that turns base metal into gold — actually, something more precious than gold. *Shaktipāt* infuses one with the essence of the Guru's own inner state: full of light, full of joy, full of enthusiasm and love for God. This grace makes a seeker pure within and without. This grace reveals the abode of God within and gives rise to love for the supreme Self and love for one another. All this glory has been given freely and permanently. Of course we feel grateful, eternally grateful. Gratitude becomes as natural as breathing.

One of the great saints of western India, Tukaram Maharaj, was a very simple man from a small village, yet he attained the highest inner state. His individuality merged with the supreme Truth. In one of his *abhangas*, his devotional songs, he offers his heartfelt gratitude to the Guru, whom he addresses as his Lord, his *deva*, saying:

> O dear Lord, my entire being had become tainted.
> Your name alone has brought the luster back to my soul.
> My heart has been cleansed by Your love.[1]

Just imagine soaking your heart over and over again in God's love. Every time you feel sad, just soak your heart in God's love. This is what the saints do. They chant God's name and they allow their hearts to be saturated with God's love. They meditate, they serve, and they chant. Again and again the saints proclaim it is God's compassionate grace that fills your heart with gratitude and brings you back to the path of righteousness. It is God's unconditional love that saves a soul. It is because God loves you that you are saved again and again.

When the mind is tainted, it is very difficult to experience gratitude. One of the simplest, easiest, and most effective ways of purifying a tainted mind is through chanting God's name. This is why you dive into chanting. Baba Muktananda used to say, "Chanting is both the means and the attainment." This is the spiritual practice that many saints prefer. Chanting will purify whatever problem you think you have. It's not that you want to throw away your problems; in truth, you can't throw them away. And you don't want to develop the tendency of walking away from your problems either. Who knows? Another one may be waiting for you just around the corner. So the best thing to do is to purify the problem and extract the best energy from it. Problems and negativities are nothing but masses of energy. What you want to do is dust off the dirt that has collected on that mass of energy. And this you do through chanting.

Do you ever pay attention to what happens to your heart, to your entire being, when you chant? It is an amazing process. You can feel God's glory shining through you. You can feel the showers of grace washing away old negativities and impurities. You begin to feel so much lighter. You must let the sound of the chant strike you like lightning. Let it go through your body, and then you can't help but love chanting. You can't help but *be* in the chant. Then gratitude will arise spontaneously. Then you will swim in the ocean of nectar.

Chanting is a very purifying force. It has the power to annihilate the effects of even the most stubborn faults. The name of God is so sweet that it permeates your being. It dissolves every ounce of bitterness and malice. If you are experiencing self-hatred or doubt or envy, you can just chant. And instead of these limitations, you will experience glory, God's glory. The name of God is a benevolent force. When you chant the Name, it actually moves through your whole being — purifying you, bestowing grace, and making you sacred.

Tukaram Maharaj chanted and chanted the name of God. Sometimes people would become annoyed with him for chanting so much. Once, some of his enemies seized hold of him and tied him up. They even put a cloth around his mouth. "Now, at last we've stopped his singing!" they thought. But still the sound "Vitthala, Vitthala, Vitthala" emanated from his being. "Vitthala" could be heard everywhere, even louder than before.

This is why the saints say, "I am not the one singing God's name. It is God who is singing the Name." This is the experience you want to have as you chant. You are not the one who is chanting; the chanting is happening of its own accord. You are being moved by the divine force. That is when you have a true experience of the chant. As long as you are thinking, "I'm chanting. Look at me! I'm chanting," then you find yourself thinking about what you will be cooking for dinner the next time you see your friends. Or you find you are feeling sorry for yourself. Or you notice some guilt arising. You are not really chanting at all. But when you let the divine force move through you, then you just watch, and the chanting happens. You don't have to do anything. You swim in the ocean of nectar. Your heart becomes flooded with gratitude. When you allow God to sing through you, you know what it means to be filled with enthusiasm and sing God's glory. Surrender your being to God and let God mold your entire being.

In another verse of his song, Tukaram Maharaj praises the Lord by saying:

> Remorse has purified me within
> and washed away the dirt of all karmas.
> I am purified because of the power of chanting.
> All my karmas are washed away.

When the hold of destiny is loosened and grace begins to play a greater role in your life, what an exhilarating experience it is! One day you suddenly realize that you have become free from old tormenting thoughts, from concepts no longer relevant to you. You find yourself free from hard feelings, venomous relationships, and all the recurring impulses you used to find so attractive. They have lost their grip on you. You are lighter. At the same time, you become aware of the compassion that has been lavished upon you. When this realization comes, tears well up in your eyes and prayers spring to your lips. All your heart wants is to praise the Lord, the supreme power that has freed you — almost without your knowing it. Have you noticed this?

Then there are times when you praise God, and you don't even know you are doing it. That is the best form of gratitude.

It is so natural to realize your great good fortune and acknowledge God's generosity. You have been blessed with sweet grace. It has changed your attitude toward life and filled you with love for God. That is why we come together again and again: to pray that the wellspring of gratitude may always remain full to the brim and continually overflow into our thoughts, our feelings, and our actions.

When a person has moved close to God, even his tears are signs of joy. Once in a question-and-answer session, Baba Muktananda said: "If you must weep, it is better to weep quietly. Weeping serves a very mysterious function. You begin to weep when you are overwhelmed by a sense of gratitude to the Lord for all the good things that you have received in your life, and those tears are very noble. Those tears are like ecstatic and joyful laughter. Sometimes when I remember all that my Guru did for me, tears come to my eyes, and that is very good."

The great saint Kabir used to say, "These tears are true holy water." He sang:

> Who will come and bathe in this holy river?
> Within my own mind I have created the Ganges.
> I have created Kashi, the sacred place.
> Who will bathe in this holy river?[2]

These tears are even better than holy water. They are sanctified by remembering the Lord, by chanting God's name, by surrendering your entire being to God in true worship.

Remembrance is an ancient spiritual practice: you remember and you acknowledge God's gifts. It is really very simple. Nothing esoteric or deep. Gratitude is your own element. It is your own gift, your own property. Nonetheless, when you experience it, it is so profound. Sometimes you get so lost in gratitude that you forget you even exist. It is natural to express gratitude, and people constantly say to one another, "Thank you, thank you. Thank you so much." "Thanks a million." "From the bottom of my heart, thank you." "*Gracias.*" "*Merçi.*" Nonetheless, the true experience of gratitude is profound. It is infinite. You cannot even see the horizon of gratitude. It spreads across the sky through eternity.

Remembrance is what allows you to experience gratitude all the time. When you begin to forget the gentle hand of God and the many great services people have performed for you, it is not just a passive oversight. In some quiet, invisible way, forgetfulness is causing you to dig your own grave. What you are doing is laying yourself open to all kinds of negativities and imbalances. And this is when you attract the so-called demons. You are letting thorny bushes choke every path you want to travel in your life. Forgetfulness isolates you and turns you away from the kingdom of God within yourself. Therefore, make it a rule to remember and acknowledge the light of grace in everyone, in every person everywhere, and in your own life and your own heart as well.

Remembrance is a practice within itself. As you remember what you have received and all the love that comes your way, you are filled with gratitude. This is one of the main purposes of satsang. This is why there are Siddha Yoga meditation ashrams and centers in many places around the world. And this is why people chant and meditate in their homes. Satsang allows you to remember and glorify the outpouring of grace in your life.

Many people attend Siddha Yoga meditation centers near their homes, so they know the importance of having regular satsang. Sometimes people drive two or three hours just to get to the center once a month. It is wonderful to have that focus, to know that on a certain day you will be going to the center to chant and meditate. You know that no matter how busy you are, on that day you will go. Just that focus, that steady remembrance, "I'll be going to the center and I'll be chanting and meditating," evokes a wonderful anticipation. "What experiences will I have when I go to the center? What message will I receive?" This remembrance keeps your heart very moist. And then you are so filled with gratitude and remembrance that everything you do is vibrant with love.

Many people who cannot attend a center for one reason or another turn their car into a mobile Siddha Yoga meditation center, a center on wheels. Baba used to call his world tours "The Siddha Yoga Meditation Tour on Wheels." In those days we moved from one place to another every three days. We would drive through the night, set up the site, and in the morning there would be a retreat — beginning with meditation at three o'clock in the morning. Then a day or two of programs or an Intensive would take place, and we would pack up again and drive through the night. The next morning we would be in a new place. There would be two hours to clean and set up the whole retreat site, and we would be ready to start again. It went on like that for two full years. It was great, it was wonderful. We loved it.

You can think of creative ways to keep your own sadhana alive, to keep your gratitude awakened. You don't have to wait for someone to say, "Hey listen, the scriptures say do this or do that." Come up with creative ways to keep your own heart moist, to keep remembrance alive and your sadhana going strong. In this way, you can encourage yourself when you feel great and also when you doubt yourself; you can inspire yourself when you feel full of energy and when you are depressed. Come up with creative ways to keep your sadhana going. This is the wonderful purpose of satsang — to be filled with enthusiasm and sing God's glory and to share this truth with others.

It is always a matter of great good fortune when a devotee is able to experience gratitude and offer thanks to the Lord. However, what can you say when the Lord Himself expresses gratitude to His devotees? Only that the ocean has overflowed its boundaries. There is a beautiful example of this in the *Bhagavad Gītā*. In Chapter Nine, Lord Krishna says to His disciple Arjuna:

> Whatever you offer — whether it is a flower, a leaf, or even a little water — I will accept it, if it is offered to Me with love.[3]

This sacred promise inspired heart-melting poetry from the great saint Jnaneshwar Maharaj. In his commentary on this verse, Jnaneshwar says:

> If a devotee, with the joy of boundless devotion, brings as an offering to Me a fruit from any tree he may choose,
>
> When he shows it to Me, however small it may be, I hold out both hands to receive it, and without even removing the stalk, I taste it respectfully.
>
> Also, if a flower is given to Me in the name of devotion, I place it in My mouth, although I should actually smell it.
>
> But why a flower, when even any leaf would be accepted? It doesn't matter whether it is fresh or dry or in any other condition.
>
> If it is offered to Me with utmost love, even though it may be a mere leaf, I take it with the same delight as a hungry man would rejoice at a drink of nectar.
>
> A leaf would do, but it may happen that one cannot be found. In that case, it isn't so difficult to find water.
>
> Water is found anywhere, without price, and one finds it even without searching for it. He who offers even that to Me in the spirit of the purest devotion,
>
> Builds for Me a temple more spacious than Vaikuntha, than heaven, and offers Me jewels more perfect than the diamond in My crown.
>
> He makes for Me many bedrooms of milk as delightful as the Milky Ocean.
>
> He gives Me sweetly scented delights such as

> camphor, sandalwood, and aloe wood. He places on Me, with his own hand, a garland of lights like the sun. . . .
>
> Tasty dishes served to Me are sweeter than nectar, and the smallest drop of water delights Me. . . .
>
> True devotion is the only thing I recognize; I make no distinction between great and small. I am ready to be welcomed by the devotion of any person.
>
> Truly, a leaf, a flower, or a fruit is for Me only a means of devotion. What I desire is complete devotion.
>
> O Arjuna, listen to Me! Gain control over your mind and then you will never forget Me, for I dwell in the temple of your heart.[4]

Lord Krishna made this divine promise, "I dwell in the temple of your heart." This is why Baba Muktananda always gave the message:

> Meditate on your own Self.
> Worship your own Self.
> Understand your own Self.
> Respect your own Self.
> God dwells within you, as you, and for you.

The presence of God in the temple of your heart gives you the power to experience this sublime feeling of gratitude. When you know it is God who dwells in your heart, what else can you feel but gratitude? Although you know many faults and mistakes have been committed through this body, God never abandons your being, never leaves His abode in your heart. God's light always shines brilliantly. To have a humble heart, filled with thankfulness all the time — that is the gift of gifts. Soak your heart in the name of God, in God's glory. Gratitude expressed in praise of the Lord is the secret of true worship. Whatever you do, do it knowing that God abides in your heart.

Most people find it easy to feel gratitude for Nature and the wonders of the natural world. You want to offer your thanks to the earth for all that it yields to nourish all living beings. You want to offer thanks to water for flowing constantly and quenching the thirst of everything that lives. You want to offer thanks to fire for burning away impurities and providing warmth. You want to offer your thanks to the wind for blowing, for keeping the atmosphere clean and sustaining your life. You want to offer thanks to the ether for its silent giving. Nature is a great giver, and she gives so silently. She never makes a show of all the things she gives you. She gives so much consolation. She is always there waiting for you, always welcoming you. It doesn't really matter whether it is raining or the sun is shining brightly. Nature gives you exactly what you need at any given moment. But do you know how to see it, how to receive it? It is like the Guru's blessings. You receive just what you are meant to receive at any given moment — but you must have the eyes to see it and the heart to accept it.

It is easy, in a way, to offer your thanks to Nature; however, when it comes to your own life, it is a little more difficult to be thankful. It is sad but true that most human beings are trained to think of what they lack and not of what they have. However, you can learn to break this habit. Instead of thinking about what you don't have, what you have not received, what hasn't happened for you within the time frame of your expectations, think of all the things that have happened. Even if you think you don't need the things you have received, still, think about them. Break the habit of constantly thinking about what you don't have. Think of the great blessings that have come your way.

Have you ever thought of being grateful to yourself? Have you thought of being grateful to your own mind? To your own heart? To your entire being? Not from the viewpoint of the ego, but simply being grateful for all that your body has put up with and the way it continually supports you in everything you want it to do. The body tolerates so much. Are you grateful to your own body, your own physical existence in this world? Not from the viewpoint of conceit and ego, but from the highest viewpoint? Are you grateful for what God has given to you?

In his book *Play of Consciousness*, Baba says: "I ask you, my dear Siddha students, did you ever look on your body with desireless love? Did you ever love it with pure Self-contemplation; with meditation, hymns, and chanting; with the *So'ham* mantra repeated on your incoming and outgoing breaths? Did you ever thank it by making vows of restraint, by offering it foods that bring it long life?"

Through the practices of Siddha Yoga you do learn to treat the body with respect and love. The body is a great gift from God that has borne up under the whiplashes of your negligence and your willfulness. No matter what your attitude is toward your body, no matter what you ask of it, the body does its best to come through for you. And how can you come through for the body? Through the practices of meditation, chanting, and contemplation; by being kind to one another; by being helpful and mindful of others' needs; by being sweet and considerate of one another; by being mindful of what the body needs; by serving one another's highest aspirations; and by filling one another's minds with good thoughts. When you practice these virtuous actions, you are giving this body the honor it deserves.

By offering your gratitude to God, the Guru, and the saints, you acknowledge that their grace has uplifted you. Through your gratitude you are also making a promise that you will continue to protect the awakened light within your own being. Truly, gratitude awakens the heart to respect and love. Gratitude moistens the heart. And when the heart is moistened in this way, the virtues grow.

Many times people tell me how they were saved from an accident, or how some great miracle has just taken place in their lives. They are full of rejoicing. And I always ask, "Did you go to the Temple and offer your gratitude to Bhagawan Nityananda? Did you meditate and offer your gratitude? Have you given something away in charity for the good that has come to you?" In the West, this is a novel idea, but in the East it is quite traditional. Any time your life is saved in a dramatic way — or in a not-so-dramatic way — you make a vow to give something in charity, to give something to a holy place or to someone who needs your assistance. The first thing to do if you have been saved like that is to promise yourself to make an offering. And, of course, you must keep that promise; otherwise it is not beneficial at all. In this way, you spread the blessings you have received, and you constantly acknowledge grace. Then, even if your mind plays tricks on you, even if it is filled with negativities and doubts, you have a very solid support, a golden support. Nothing can shake your faith; you are established in it. Every time you offer your gratitude, you are making an attempt to remember God's glory, to remember what you have received.

A poet-saint of Maharashtra offered his gratitude in this way:

The saints are generous oceans of grace.
How do I express my gratitude for their kindness?
The saints are so generous.
How will I ever offer my gratitude?

They always care for my welfare
and give me the treasure of the inner Self
and constantly look after me.
Grace is so abundant.

They keep me aware of the Self
and bring me face-to-face with God Himself.

Swami says, I prostrate before them in gratitude.
What else can I do?
It is so impossible to repay this debt.[5]

Take a few minutes now and count your blessings. Be grateful to your own body. Be grateful to your own mind. Don't be hard on your mind. If it has bad thoughts and negative judgments, it is all right. Be grateful to your mind: it has brought you to the spiritual path, it is your friend. Remember that the Lord said, "I dwell in the temple of your heart." Again and again become aware of the divine light that blazes in your own heart.

Remember all the love you have received in this universe, all the people who make your life shine. Remember Nature who has taught you many lessons and given you divine hints about yourself. Don't think of what you have not achieved. Remember the things that have come your way — some asked for, some not. God's grace is given freely. It is immeasurable.

The Lord made a divine promise: "I dwell in the temple of your heart." Believe in it. Embrace it. Allow your heart to be moistened with the nectar of gratitude. Let gratitude wash away all the tiredness, all the impurities, and all the karmas. Remember all the goodness that permeates your life.

Remember. Remember the grace and blessings. Never forget the divine source from which you receive everything. Be filled with enthusiasm and sing God's glory.

With great respect, with great love, I welcome you all with all my heart.

*Sadgurunāth mahārāj kī jay!*

# EPILOGUE

With great respect, with great love, I welcome you all with all my heart.

It is certain that we will see one another over and over again. We will be with one another in many different ways. No matter where you go, you will be chanting and we will be chanting. You will be repeating the mantra and we will be repeating the mantra. You will be doing seva and we will be doing seva. You will be meditating and we will be meditating. You will be having satsang and we will be having satsang. And who knows? You may be sending birds our way, and we may be sending birds your way. And the birds who have heard us singing the mantras will come and sing them to you. And the birds who hear you singing the mantras will come and tell us about it. And who knows? The leaves that have been falling here will fly to your place, and the leaves that have been with you will fly to our place. Who knows how we will be talking to one another and how we will be exchanging our love for one another? Many times people from here will come to the places where you are. They will bring messages from us and they will bring their experiences. And the people who have been with you will be coming to us and bringing your messages. We will be staying in touch in many different ways.

An ample number of things will keep us together. We will be together in our thoughts, our feelings, and of course, our dreams. Many of you do come into my dreams, and it is really very beautiful. When you are interacting with me in the waking state, in your physical forms, sometimes you are shy, or hesitant, or a little reticent. But in my dreams it is not that way at all, and it is so sweet. You are completely open and forthright. It is as though we are in a different world, in the world of Satya Yuga, the Age of Truth, where no one feels barriers or differences. The scriptures tell us it is disparity that creates fear, it is a sense of differences that creates uneasiness. But in my dreams we are in Satya Yuga, and it is a beautiful place to be. It is like the space we experience in meditation.

So we will be in touch with one another in many different ways. No one has to feel, "I am going through this sadhana all by myself. Where is my God? Where is my Guru? Where are the other seekers? Who is going to help me?" You don't have to feel like that. Truly, there is so much support in your life. You just need to become aware of it.

Recently someone asked me: How can a person know the Guru's help is always there? How can people not feel they are going through hard times all by themselves? The truth of the matter is, the Guru's help is always there, and it comes in innumerable ways. You don't have to be looking for the Guru's form to appear before you, coming toward you with an extended hand, picking you up and stroking your face. Help comes in many different ways: through other people, through events in your life, through your own insights. So don't think that help should come only through the physical form of the Guru. Help comes in the form of the *shakti*, in the form of grace. It may be in someone's words. Even in just one word that someone says to you — the Guru's help is there in that one word.

Experiment with this in your life. See how the Guru's help comes to you, in what form. It will be a delightful practice. It will be enlightening to experience the Guru's help coming to you in many different ways: when your heart is softened by someone's kind word, when all of a sudden you remember the experience of God you had when you were four and a half years old. Just like that, the memory comes, and you say, "Ah! That's the experience that has seen me through." So let it be your sadhana experiment to see how the Guru's help comes to you. Experiment with this. How and when does the Guru's help come? Observe how this practice changes your perception, how it accelerates your sadhana, and how because of it, you become someone very special in your world. You will begin to see that you are loved, that you are so valuable in this creation.

For a few moments now become quiet and allow yourselves to receive whatever you must receive. Having done sadhana, having given yourself to spiritual practices, understand that your body has become the temple of God. Your body is imbued with beautiful vibrations of meditation, with the vibrations of God's love. Allow your entire body to relax. Allow your mind to relax.

Acknowledge to yourself how special your life is, how precious it is. Your body is the temple of God. Empty yourself completely. Whatever the Siddhas, the perfected Masters, want to instill in you, accept it, embrace it with total respect and love. Have no expectations. Empty yourself completely. Allow them to instill their *mahāprasād*, their great blessing, in your being. Allow them to anoint your entire being inside and out with their light, with their wisdom, with their love. Empty yourself completely. Just as a child melts into the arms of its mother, allow yourself to melt into the arms of the Siddhas, the great ones, who are compassionate, who bestow grace. Allow the Siddhas to instill whatever they want into your being. Accept their *mahāprasād* with total respect, total love.

Remember to do this experiment, to see in how many ways the Guru's help comes to you: in how many grand and little ways, in how many visible and invisible ways, in how many tangible and intangible ways. Really do this experiment. It will be delightful and enlightening, and you will see how truly loved you are. Be filled with enthusiasm and sing God's glory.

With great respect, with great love, I welcome you all with all my heart.

*Sadgurunāth mahārāj kī jay!*

# *Notes on Sources*

Most of the poetry by the saints of the Indian tradition was newly translated for the talks presented in this volume. Many of the scriptural quotations were also freshly rendered, drawing from the original Sanskrit texts as well as the following sources in English:

Kisari Mohan Ganguli, translator, *The Mahābhārata of Krishna-Dwaipayana Vyasa*, Vols. I-XII (New Delhi: Munshiram Manoharlal Publishers Pvt., Ltd., 1981).

Ram Kumar Rai, translator, *Kulārnava Tantra* (Varanasi: Prachya Prakashay, 1983).

Winthrop Sargeant, translator, *The Bhagavad Gītā* (Albany: State University of New York Press, 1984).

Hari Ram Shastri, translator, *The Rāmāyana of Valmiki*, Vols. I-III (London: Shantisadan, 1962).

Jaideva Singh, translator, *The Yoga of Delight, Wonder, and Astonishment: A Translation of the Vijñāna-bhairava* (Delhi: Motilal Banarsidass, 1991). First published in the U.S.A. by State University of New York Press, Albany.

Swami Tapasyananda, translator, *Śrīmad Bhāgavatam: The Holy Book of God*, Vols. I-IV (Madras: Sri Ramakrishna Math, 1980).

Rai Bahadur Srisa Chandra Vasu, translator, *The Śiva Samhitā* (New Delhi: Oriental Books Reprint Corp., 1979).

Swami Vijnananada, translator *Śrīmad Devī Bhāgavatam* (New Delhi: Oriental Books Reprint Corp., 1986).

Robert Bly, renderings, *The Kabir Book: Forty-Four of the Ecstatic Poems of Kabir* (Boston: Beacon Press, 1971).

# *Permission to Quote Sources*

We gratefully acknowledge permission to quote passages from the following sources, in order of their appearance in the book:

Constantina Rhodes Bailly, *Meditations on Shiva: The Shivastotravali of Utpaladeva* (Albany: State University of New York Press, ©1995). Reprinted by permission of the State University of New York Press.

Excerpt from "A Blessing" by James Wright, from *The Norton Anthology of Poetry*, revised edition (New York and London: W. W. Norton & Co., 1975), pp. 606-07. Reprinted by permission.

Swami Kripananda, *Jnaneshwar's Gītā: A Rendering of the Jñāneshwarī* (Albany: State University of New York Press, ©1989). Reprinted by permission of the State University of New York Press.

Gia-Fu Feng and Jane English, translators, *Tao Te Ching* (New York and Toronto: Random House, Vintage Books Edition, 1972), verse 76. Reprinted by permission.

# *Guide to Sanskrit Pronunciation*

### *Vowels*

Sanskrit vowels are categorized as either long or short. In English transliteration, the long vowels are marked with a macron above the letter and are pronounced twice as long as the short vowels. The vowels *e* and *o* are always pronounced as long vowels.

| Short: | Long: | |
|---|---|---|
| *a* as in c*u*p | *ā* as in c*a*lm | *e* as in s*a*ve |
| *i* as in g*i*ve | *ī* as in s*ee*n | *o* as in ph*o*ne |
| *u* as in f*u*ll | *ū* as in sch*oo*l | *ai* as in *ai*sle |
| *ṛ* as in w*ri*tten | | *au* as in c*ow* |

### *Consonants*

The main difference between Sanskrit and English pronunciation of consonants is in the aspirated letters. In Sanskrit these are pronounced with a definite *h* sound. The following list covers variations of pronunciation for most of the Sanskrit consonants found in this book:

| | |
|---|---|
| *ḥ* as in the German a*ch* | *ṃ* is a strong nasal *m* |
| *c* as in su*ch* | *ṅ* as in si*ng* |
| *ch* as in *ch*ew | *ñ* as in ca*ny*on |
| *jh* as in he*dgeh*og | *ṇ* as in no*n*e |
| *th* as in boa*th*ouse | *n* as in s*n*ake |
| *ṭh* as in an*th*ill | *ś* as in bu*sh* |
| *ḍh* as in roa*dh*ouse | *ṣ* as in *sh*ine |
| *dh* as in a*dh*ere | *s* as in *s*upreme |
| *ph* as in loo*ph*ole | *kṣ* as in au*ct*ion |
| *bh* as in clu*bh*ouse | |

The full transliteration for each Sanskrit term is included in the Glossary of Texts and Terms and in the Notes. For a detailed pronunciation guide, see *The Nectar of Chanting*, published by SYDA Foundation.

# *Notes*

## Chapter One: Be Filled with Enthusiasm and Sing God's Glory

*January 1, 1996*

1. This and the subsequent passage in this paragraph are from Mark S. G. Dyczkowski, *The Doctrine of Vibration: An Analysis of the Doctrines and Practices of Kashmir Shaivism* (Albany: State University of New York Press, 1987), p. 149.

2. *Rāmāyaṇa*
   *sā hānis-tan-mahac-chidraṃ sa mohaḥ sa ca vibhramaḥ /*
   *yan-muhūrtaṃ kṣaṇaṃ vāpi vāsudevaṃ na kīrtayet //*

## Chapter Two: We Are Born of God's Ecstasy

*May 4-5, 1996*

1. *Śivastotrāvalī 14.12, 14.18, 13.15*
   *jaya sarva-jagan-nyasta-sva-mudrā-vyakta-vaibhava /*
   *jayātma-dāna-paryanta-viśveśvara maheśvara //*

   *jaya mohāndhakārāndha-jīva-lokaika-dīpaka /*
   *jaya prasupta-jagatī-jāgarūkādhipūruṣa //*

   *sphārayasy-akhilam-ātmanā sphuran*
   *viśvam-āmṛśasi rūpam-āmṛśan /*
   *yat-svayaṃ nija-rasena ghūrṇase*
   *tat-samullasati bhāva-maṇḍalam //*

   English translation: Constantina Rhodes Bailly, *Meditations on Shiva: The Shivastotravali of Utpaladeva* (Albany: State University of New York Press, 1995), pp. 91, 93, 86.

2. *Rāmāyaṇa 3.63.19 (āraṇya-kāṇḍa, sarga 63)*
   *śokaṃ visṛjyādya dhṛtiṃ bhajasva sotsāhā cāstu*
   *vimārgaṇe 'syāḥ /*
   *utsāhavanto hi narā na loke sīdanti*
   *karmasv-atiduṣkareṇa //*

3. Brahmananda:
   *bāhira ḍhūṇḍha na jā mata sajanī //*

## Chapter Three: The Wellspring of Enthusiasm

*June 29-30, 1996*

1. *Tantrāloka 3.68cd-69*
   *ānanda-śaktiḥ saivoktā yato viśvaṃ visṛjyate //*
   *parāparāt-paraṃ tattvaṃ saiṣā devī nigadyate /*
   *tat-sāraṃ tac-ca hṛdayaṃ sa visargaḥ paraḥ prabhuḥ //*

2. *Amṛtānubhava 1.8*

3. From "A Blessing" by James Wright, reprinted from *The Norton Anthology of Poetry*, revised edition (New York and London: W. W. Norton & Co., 1975), pp. 606-07.

4. *Śiva-saṃhitā 4.13*
   *suptā guru-prasādena yadā jāgarti kuṇḍalī /*
   *tadā sarvāṇi padmāni bhidyante granthayo 'pi ca //*

5. The unstruck sound, *anāhata nada*, is the inner divine sound that can be heard in many different forms in deep meditation. The inner sound is referred to as "unstruck" because, unlike sounds in the physical universe, it is not the result of two objects meeting — for instance, the striking of wood on metal or the passage of air over vocal chords — but issues directly from the innermost core of one's being.

6. Once a meditator has gone beyond the five elements (earth, water, fire, air, and ether) and the twenty-five principles of creation (the *tattvas*, or specific levels of subtlety in the universe as identified in Indian philosophy) then he or she has "won the field," that is, achieved the goal. In Chapter 13 of the *Bhagavad Gītā*, there is a classic depiction of one's physical body and psychic instrument as a field in which one's actions and thoughts, like planted seeds, have predictable outcomes. To use this body to transcend limited consciousness is, truly, to have mastered the field.

7. Author unknown:
   *magana hoya caḍha gayo gagana pe adhara dhāra dhyānā //*

## Chapter Four: The True Companion Within

*June 23, 1996*

1. *Ātmabodha 66*
   *śravaṇādībhir-uddīpta-jñānāgni-paritāpitaḥ /*
   *jīvas-sarva-malān-muktaḥ svarṇavad-dyotate svayam //*

2. *Bhagavadgītā 4.38*
   *na hi jñānena sadṛśaṃ pavitram-iha vidyate /*
   *tat-svayaṃ yoga-saṃsiddhaḥ kālenātmani vindati //*

3. This is a graphic metaphor indicating that those whose lives are spent in worldly pursuits are caught in the end on the wheel of death and rebirth; that is, when death comes to them, they must reap the consequences of the

way they have lived. Tulsidas is saying that if even the most powerful of kings has no power over death, then how could the common people to whom he addresses these lines think they will fare differently? The great souls who vanquish death are those who have spent their lives remembering the Lord and whose consciousness, when leaving the body, merges with the Lord.

4. Tulsidas:
*tāṃbe so pīṭhi mānahu tana pāyo //*

5. Prabhudas:
*chailā banakara phirai bāga me dhara pagaḍī me phūla //*

6. Kabir:
*tana chūṭe jiva milana kahata hai so saba jhūṭhi āsā //*

7. *Tantrāloka 26.60-61*
*citaḥ svātantrya-sāratvāt-tasyānanda-ghanatvataḥ //*
*kriyā syāphan-mayī-bhūtyai chadayāthādadāyibhiḥ //*

8. Jnaneshwar Maharaj:
*avaghāci saṃsāra sukhācā karīna ānande bharīna tinhī loka //*

## Chapter Five: Freedom of Speech

*July 4, 1996*

1. Bible, Book of Proverbs 10.19

2. Sundardas, from the *bhajan* beginning:
*kāka aru rāsabha ulūka jaba bolata hai //*

3. *Jñāneśvarī 13.260, 262, 264-72*

   English translation: Swami Kripananda, *Jnaneshwar's Gītā: A Rendering of the Jñāneshwarī* (Albany: State University of New York Press, 1989), p. 193.

4. Bholenath:
*yaha viśva śiva kī vātikā hai saira karane ke liye //*

## Chapter Six: Discarding the Burden of Self-Hatred

*July 6, 1996*

1. Ravidas:
*prabhujī tuma candana hama pānī //*

   When Ravidas says that the Lord is the sandalwood and he, the devotee, is the water, he is referring to Indian rituals in which sandalwood dust is mixed with water to make a ceremonial paste; it is the sandalwood that adds fragrance. When he says that the Lord is the cloud and he the *chātaka* bird and the Lord is the moon and he the *chakora* bird, he is referring to the Indian tradition in which the *chātaka* is thought to drink only the purest rainwater and the *chakora* to exist on the nectar of moonbeams.

2. Arthur Green and Barry W. Holtz, editors and translators, *Your Word Is Fire: The Hasidic Masters on Contemplative Prayer* (New York: Paulist Press, 1977), pp. 16-17.

## Chapter Seven: The Jewel of Constancy

*July 7, 1996*

1. Shankaracharya:
   *prātaḥ smarāmi hṛdi saṃsphurad-ātma-tattvaṃ*
   *sac-cit-sukhaṃ parama-haṃsa-gatiṃ turīyam /*
   *yat-svapna-jāgara-suṣuptam-avaiti nityaṃ*
   *tad-brahma-niṣkalam-ahaṃ na ca bhūta-saṅghaḥ //*

2. Brahmananda:
   *prabhu mere dila me sadā yāda ānā //*

3. Dadu Deena Dayal:
   *ham bisarai tyom tū na bisārai /*
   *ham bigarai pai tū na bigārai //*

4. *Viṣṇusahasranāma 8*
   *anādī-nidhanaṃ viṣṇuṃ sarva-loka-maheśvaram /*
   *lokādhyakṣaṃ stuvan-nityaṃ sarva-duḥkhātigo bhavet //*

5. *Śrīmad-devī-bhāgavatam 7.37.15 (devīgītā)*
   *parānuraktyā mām-eva cintayed-yo 'tandritaḥ /*
   *svābhedenaiva māṃ nityaṃ jānāti na vibhedataḥ //*

6. *Śrīmadbhāgavatam 1.2.18*
   *naṣṭa-prāyeṣv-abhadreṣu nityaṃ bhāgavat-sevayā /*
   *bhagavaty-uttama-śloke bhaktir-bhavati naiṣṭhikī //*

7. *Kulārṇavatantra 15.111*
   *viśvāsāstikya-karuṇā-śraddhā-niyama-niścayaiḥ /*
   *santoṣautsukya-dharmādi-guṇair-yukto japen-naraḥ //*

8. *Bhagavadgītā 8.14*
   *ananya-cetāḥ satataṃ yo māṃ smarati nityaśaḥ /*
   *tasyāhaṃ sulabhaḥ pārtha nitya-yuktasya yoginaḥ //*

9. Brahmananda:
   *prabhu mere dila me sadā yāda ānā //*

## Chapter Eight: Patience, the Vitalizing Power of Enthusiasm

*July 29, 1996*

1. From the Kabir *bhajan* beginning:
   *mana lāgo mero yār phakīrī me //*

## Chapter Nine: Forgiveness Sings the Glory of the Heart

*July 21, 1996*

1. *Śiva-mānasa-pūjā 5*
   *kara-caraṇa-kṛtaṃ vāk-kāyajaṃ karmajaṃ vā*
   *śravaṇa-nayanajaṃ vā mānasaṃ vāparādham /*
   *vihitam-avihitaṃ vā sarvam-etat-kṣamasva*
   *jaya jaya karuṇābdhe śrī-mahādeva śambho //*

2. Brahmananda:
   *prabhu mere dila me sadā yāda ānā //*

3. Kabir:
   *āvata gārī eka hai ulaṭata hoya aneka //*

## Chapter Ten: The Marvelous Balance of Gentleness

*August 3, 1996*

1. *Atharvaveda 19.1.1*
   *sa saṃ sravantu nadyaḥ saṃ vātāḥ saṃ patatriṇaḥ /*
   *yajñam-imaṃ vardhayatā giraḥ saṃsravyeṇa haviṣā juhomi //*

   English translation: Pandit Satyakam Vidyalankar, *The Holy Vedas* (Delhi: Clarion Books), p. 123

2. *Śrīmadbhāgavatam 5.18.9*
   *svasty-astu viśvasya khalaḥ prasīdatāṃ dhyāyantu bhūtāni*
   *śivaṃ mitho dhiyā /*
   *manaś-ca bhadraṃ bhajatād-adhokṣaja āveśyatāṃ no*
   *matir-apy-ahaitukī //*

3. From the Upanishads of the *Śukla Yajurveda* (*Bṛhadāraṇyaka*, *Īśa*, *Jābāla*, *Paiṅgala*, and *Sūrya Upaniṣad*):
   *oṃ pūrṇam-adaḥ pūrṇam-idaṃ pūrṇāt-pūrṇam-udacyate /*
   *pūrṇasya pūrṇam-ādāya pūrṇam-evāvaśiṣyate //*

4. Tukaram:
   *maū meṇāhūna āmhī viṣṇudāsa //*

5. English translation: Gia-Fu Feng and Jane English, translators, *Tao Te Ching* (New York and Toronto: Random House, Vintage Books Edition, 1972), verse 76.

## Chapter Eleven: Untangling the Mesh of Envy

*August 4, 1996*

1. This *bhajan* was written by one of Swami Muktananda's devotees, the singer Hari Om Sharan:
   *mailī cādara oḍha ke kaise dvāra tumhāre āū //*

2. *Kaṭhopaniṣad 1.2.1-3*

3. *Vijñānabhairava 96*
*jhagitīcchāṃ samutpannām-avalokya śamaṃ nayet /*
*yata eva samudbhūtā tatas-tatraiva līyate //*

4. Rama Tirtha:
*tere karam se benayāj kaunasī śai milī nahī //*

## Chapter Twelve: Seva Creates a Pond of Nectar

*August 17, 1996*

1. *Bhakti-sūtra 36*
*avyāvṛta-bhajanāt //*

2. *Ṛgveda 5.37.5*
*puṣyāt kṣeme abhi yoge bhavāty ubhe vṛtau saṃyatī saṃ jayāti /*
*priyaḥ sūrye priyo agnā bhavāti ya indrāya sutasomo dādāśat //*

   English translation: Vidyalankar, *The Holy Vedas*, p. 114.

3. Janabai:
*nāhī kelī tujhī sevā duḥkha vāṭe mājhe jīvā //*

4. *Jṇāneśvarī 13.428-29*

   English translation: Swami Kripananda's rendering, *Jnaneshwar's Gītā*, p. 197.

5. *Rāmāyaṇa*
*deha-buddhyā nu dāso 'haṃ jīva-buddhyā svadaṃśakaḥ /*
*ātmā-buddhyā tvam-evāham-iti me niścita-matiḥ //*

## Chapter Thirteen: Gratitude, the Gift of Remembrance

*August 18, 1996*

1. Tukaram:
*jhālī hotī kāyā bahu malīṇa devarāyā //*

2. Kabir:
*tīratha kaun kare hamāre tīratha kaun kare //*

3. *Bhagavadgītā 9.26*
*patraṃ puṣpaṃ phalaṃ toyaṃ yo me bhaktyā prayacchati /*
*tad-ahaṃ bhakty-upahṛtam-aśnāmi prayatātmanaḥ //*

4. *Jñāneśvarī 9:378-87, 389, 391-93*

   English translation: Swami Kripananda's rendering, *Jnaneshwar's Gītā*, p. 125.

5. Swami Swarupananda:
*santa te udāra kṛpece sāgara //*

# *Glossary of Poets, Philosophers, and Sages*

**ABHINAVAGUPTA**
(993-1015) A commentator and exponent of Kashmir Shaivism in the lineage of Vasugupta and Somananda, he is the author of *Īshwara Pratyabhijñā Vimarshinī* and *Tantrāloka.*

**AKBAR**
(1542-1605) A Moghul emperor who consolidated an extensive Indian empire. His administrative skills, benevolent nature, and interest in culture and religion endeared him to his people.

**BA'AL SHEM TOV**
Rabbi Yisra'el ben Eli'ezer, known as the Ba'al Shem Tov ("master of the good name"), founded the Hassidim, a Jewish sect, in eighteenth-century Poland. His teaching stories capture his passionate, mystical love for God and the understanding that the highest religion is union with God, here and now.

**BHOLENATH**
A nineteenth-century poet-saint of Uttar Pradesh, who composed *bhajans* and a number of poetical works on Vedanta, including the *Siddha Gītā* and *Vedānta Chandāvali.*

**BRAHMANANDA**
A nineteenth-century Rajasthani saint who lived in Pushkar, where he was a devout worshiper at the only temple in India dedicated to Brahma. A great poet and yogi, he wrote *Īshwara Darshana* ("the vision of God"), proclaiming that God is manifest. He also expressed his learning and wisdom in the form of ecstatic *bhajans.*

**DADU DEENA DAYAL**
(1544-1603) A learned poet-saint of northern India whose ecstatic experiences of God are recorded in his poetry, *Anabhaivani* and *Kāyabeli*, and whose *bhajans* are still sung today by the sadhus of the mission he established.

**FRANCIS, SAINT**
(1181-1226) A Christian saint and mystic from the Italian town of Assisi, revered for his simplicity, gentleness, and love of nature.

**GORAKHNATH**
The eleventh-century Guru of Gahininath, who initiated Nivritti, Jnaneshwar's older brother and Guru. Gorakhnath, one of the nine Nath masters, received initiation from Matsyendranath, the first Guru of the Nath lineage.

**IBRAHIM, HAZRAT**
An eighth-century king of Balkh (now in Afghanistan). One day while hunting, he heard a voice reminding him about death; the impact of this inner message was so strong that he renounced his kingdom to live as an ascetic.

**JANABAI**
A thirteenth-century saint who was the disciple and house servant of the Maharashtrian poet-saint Namdev. It is said that Lord Krishna was so moved by her devotion that He appeared to Janabai and helped her with her work.

**JNANESHWAR MAHARAJ**
(1275-1296) Foremost among the poet-saints of Maharashtra. His older brother, Nivrittinath, was his Guru. At the age of twenty-one, Jnaneshwar took live *samādhi* (a yogi's voluntary departure from the body) in Alandi where, to this day, his *samādhi* shrine attracts thousands of seekers. His best known work is *Jñāneshwarī*, a commentary in Marathi verse on the *Bhagavad Gītā.*

**KABIR**
(1440-1518) A great poet-saint and mystic who lived as a simple weaver in Benares. His poems describe the universality of the Self, the greatness of the Guru, and the nature of true spirituality. They are still studied and sung all over the world.

**MUKTANANDA, SWAMI**
(1908-1982) Swami Chidvilasananda's Guru, often referred to as Baba. This great Siddha brought the powerful and rare initiation known as *shaktipāt* to the West on the command of his own Guru, Bhagawan Nityananda.

**NAMDEV**
(1270-1350) A poet-saint of the village of Pandharpur in Maharashtra and friend of Jnaneshwar Maharaj. Namdev composed ecstatic *abhangas* to Vitthal, a form of Lord Krishna.

**NANAK, GURU**
(1469-1538) Founder and first Guru of the Sikh religion. He lectured widely, spreading liberal religious and social doctrines including opposition to both the caste system and the division between Hindus and Muslims.

**NARADA**
A divine seer who was a great devotee and servant of Lord Vishnu. Narada appears in many of the Puranas and is the author of the *Bhakti Sūtras*, the authoritative text on the path of devotion to God.

**NITYANANDA, BHAGAWAN**
(d. 1961) A great Siddha Master, Swami Muktananda's Guru, also known as Bade ("elder") Baba. He was a born Siddha, living his entire life in the highest state of Consciousness. In both Gurudev Siddha Peeth in Ganeshpuri, India, and Shree Muktananda Ashram in South Fallsburg, New York, Swami Muktananda has dedicated a temple of meditation to honor Bhagawan Nityananda.

**PATANJALI**
A fourth-century sage and the author of the famous *Yoga Sūtras*, the exposition of one of the six orthodox philosophies of India and the authoritative text of the path of *rāja yoga*, the "kingly path," the path of meditation.

RAMA TIRTHA
(1873-1906) A distinguished professor of mathematics, who, out of his longing for God, withdrew to the Himalayas and attained enlightenment. Rama Tirtha wrote many beautiful poems in the Urdu language, and in the last years of his life he lectured on Vedanta in Japan and the United States.

RAVIDAS
A fifteenth-century poet-saint who worked as a cobbler in Benares, India.

SHANKARACHARYA
(788-820) One of the most celebrated of India's philosophers and sages, he traveled throughout the country expounding the philosophy of Advaita ("nondual") Vedanta. Among his many works is the *Viveka Chūdāmani*, "The Crest Jewel of Discrimination."

SHEIKH SA'DI
(1200-1291) A renowned Sufi scholar and the author of the *Gulistān*, a collection of allegorical tales.

SUNDARDAS
(1596-1689) A poet-saint born in Rajasthan. The main collection of his *bhajans* is the *Sundar Granthavāti.*

TIRUMULAR
An eighth-century saint from Tamil in South India; one of the Shaiva poet-saints known as Nayanars. Tirumular is best known for his 3,000-verse treatise, *Tirumantiram*, which translates and interprets Shaiva scriptures into the Tamil language.

TUKARAM MAHARAJ
(1608-1650) A poet-saint who was a grocer in the village of Dehu in Maharashtra. He received initiation in a dream. Tukaram wrote thousands of *abhangas*, many of which describe his spiritual struggles and visionary experiences.

TULSIDAS
(1532-1623) The poet-saint of North India who wrote the *Rāmācharitmānas* or *Tulsi Rāmāyana* in Hindi. This life story of Rama is still one of the most popular scriptures in India.

UTPALADEVA
A tenth-century Shaiva poet and philosopher, one of the earliest exponents of Kashmir Shaivism. Foremost among his works is the *Īshwara Pratyabhijñā Kārikās*, "Stanzas on the Recognition of God," which describes the recognition of one's true identity as Shiva.

# Glossary of Texts and Terms

ABHANGA [*abhaṅga*]
A devotional song composed in the Marathi language that expresses the longing and love of a devotee for God.

ABSOLUTE, THE
The highest Reality; supreme Consciousness; the pure, untainted, changeless Truth.

AMRITANUBHAVA [*amṛtānubhava*]
(*lit.*, nectar of Self-awareness) A lyrical text, written in verse by Jnaneshwar Maharaj, on the nature of the supreme Lord (Shiva) and his power of creation (Shakti).

ANAHATA CHAKRA *See* CHAKRA.

ANANDA SHAKTI [*ānandaśakti*]
The power of absolute bliss.

APASMARA [*apasmara*]
Ignorance; the state in which one forgets one's identity with the Divine.

ARATI [*āratī*]
1) A ritual act of worship during which a flame, symbolic of the individual soul, is waved before the form of a deity, sacred being, or image that embodies the light of Consciousness. 2) The name of the morning and evening prayer that is sung with the waving of lights, in honor of Bhagawan Nityananda twice each day in Siddha Yoga ashrams.

ARJUNA [*arjuna*]
The third of the five Pandava brothers and one of the heroes of the *Mahābhārata*, considered to be the greatest warrior of all. He was the friend and devotee of Lord Krishna. It was to Arjuna that the Lord revealed the knowledge of the *Bhagavad Gītā.*

ASANA [*āsana*]
1) A seat or mat on which one sits for meditation. 2) A hatha yoga posture practiced to strengthen and purify the body.

ASHRAM [*āśrama*]
The dwelling place of a Guru or saint; a monastic retreat site where seekers engage in spiritual practices and study the sacred teachings of yoga. *See also* GURUKULA.

ATHARVA VEDA [*atharvaveda*]
One of the four fundamental scriptures of India, consisting primarily of protective healing formulas and prayers.

ATMA BALA SPARSHA
[*ātmā-bala-sparśa*]
Inspiration coming from contact with the strength, splendor, and brilliance of the Self.

ATMABODHA [*ātmabodha*]
(*lit.*, Self-knowledge) A short treatise on Vedanta by Shankaracharya, consisting of sixty-eight verses, teaching that one's true Self is the Self of all beings. *See also* VEDANTA.

ATMAN [*ātman*]
Divine Consciousness residing in the individual; the supreme Self; the soul.

**BHAGAVAD GITA** [*bhagavadgītā*]
(*lit.*, song of God) One of the world's spiritual treasures and an essential scripture of India; a portion of the *Mahābhārata* in which Lord Krishna instructs his disciple Arjuna on the nature of the universe, God, and the supreme Self. *See also* ARJUNA; KRISHNA; MAHABHARATA.

**BHAJAN**
In Hindi, a devotional song in praise of God.

**BHAKTA** [*bhaktā*]
A devotee, a lover of God; a follower of *bhakti yoga*, the path of love and devotion.

**BHAKTI SUTRAS** [*bhakti-sūtra*]
The classic scripture on devotion to God, composed by the sage Narada.

**BHASMA** [*bhasma*]
Ash from a sacred fire ritual, charged with the power of mantra. *Bhasma* is used to draw three horizontal stripes on the forehead and other parts of the body, representing the three qualities of nature reduced to ash by spiritual practices and the power of grace.

**BRAHMA** [*brahmā*]
The absolute Reality manifested as the active creator of the universe, personified as one of the three gods of the Hindu trinity.

**BRAHMA GRANTHI** *See* GRANTHI.

**BRAHMAN** [*brahman*]
The Vedic term for the absolute Reality.

**CHAKRA(S)** [*cakra*]
(*lit.*, wheel) A center of energy located in the subtle body where the *nādīs* (subtle nerve channels) converge, like the spokes of a wheel. Six major chakras lie within the *sushumnā nādī*, the central channel. They are *mūlādhāra* at the base of the spine; *svādhishthāna* at the root of the reproductive organs; *manipūra* at the navel; *anāhata*, the "lotus of the heart"; *vishuddha* at the throat; and *ājñā* between the eyebrows. When awakened, *kundalinī shakti* flows upward from the *mūlādhāra* to the seventh chakra, the *sahasrāra*, at the crown of the head. *See also* KUNDALINI; SHAKTIPAT; SUSHUMNA NADI.

**CHAMATKARA** [*camatkāra*]
Wonder; astonishment; surprise.

**CHITI SHAKTI** [*citiśakti*]
The power of universal Consciousness; the creative aspect of God portrayed as the universal Mother, the Goddess, who is known by many names.

**DARSHAN** [*darśana*]
(*lit.*, to have sight of; viewing) A glimpse or vision of a saint; being in the presence of a holy being; seeing God or an image of God.

**DEVI GITA** [*devīgītā*]
(*lit.*, song of the Goddess) A portion of the *Shrīmad Devī Bhāgavatam*, a Purana devoted to the Goddess.

**DHARANA** [*dhāraṇā*]
A centering technique that leads one to the experience of God within.

**DHARMA** [*dharma*]
(*lit.*, what holds together) Essential duty; the law of righteousness; living in accordance with the divine will. The highest dharma is to recognize the Truth in one's own heart.

**DURGA** [*durgā*]
(*lit.*, hard to conquer) The fierce aspect of the universal Shakti or divine Mother, who destroys limitations and evil tendencies. She is often depicted as the eight-armed warrior goddess who rides a tiger and carries weapons.

**DURYODHANA** [*duryodhana*]
The wicked leader of the Kauravas in their war with the Pandavas, which is described in the *Mahābhārata* epic.

DVESHA [*dveṣa*]
Hatred; repugnance; enmity; aversion.

GANESHA [*gaṇeṣa*]
The elephant-headed god, also known as Ganapati. The son of Lord Shiva and Goddess Parvati, he is worshiped at the beginning of any undertaking, as well as in many festivals, as the god of wisdom, the destroyer of sorrows, and the remover of obstacles.

GANGES
The most sacred river of India, the Ganges, traditionally known as the goddess Ganga, is said to descend from heaven through Lord Shiva's matted hair. On earth, it flows down from the Himalayas, across all of North India to the Bay of Bengal. It is believed that all sins are purified by a dip in its holy waters.

GRANTHI(S) [*granthi*]
A mass of karmic traces, occurring at three significant junctures in the subtle system along the *sushumnā nādī*. These knots, which must be pierced by the awakened *kundalinī*, are *brahmā granthi* in the *mūlādhāra chakra*, *vishnu granthi* in the *anāhata chakra*, and *rudra granthi* in the *ājñā chakra*. *See also* CHAKRA; KHECHARI MUDRA; SUSHUMNA NADI.

GURU [*guru*]
(*lit.*, *gu*, darkness; *ru*, light) A spiritual Master who has attained oneness with God and who is therefore able both to initiate seekers and to guide them on the spiritual path to liberation. A Guru is also required to be learned in the scriptures and must belong to a lineage of Masters. *See also* SHAKTIPAT.

GURU GITA [*gurugītā*]
(*lit.*, song of the Guru) A sacred text; a garland of mantras that describe the nature of the Guru, the Guru-disciple relationship, and meditation on the Guru. In Siddha Yoga meditation ashrams, the *Guru Gītā* is chanted every morning.

GURUDEV SIDDHA PEETH
(*lit.*, abode of the perfected beings) The main Siddha Yoga ashram, located in Ganeshpuri, India; the site of the *samādhi* shrine of Swami Muktananda.

GURUKULA [*gurukula*]
(*lit.*, family or group of the Master) In Vedic times, spiritual aspirants would serve the Guru at his house or ashram for a period of time, studying the scriptures and practicing self-inquiry and other spiritual disciplines under the guidance of the Master. Siddha Yoga ashrams are modeled on these *gurukulas* of old. *See also* ASHRAM.

HANUMAN [*hanumān*]
A huge white monkey, son of the Wind, and one of the heroes of the *Rāmāyana*. Hanuman's unparalleled strength was exceeded only by his perfect devotion to Lord Rama, for whom he performed many acts of magic and daring.

HATHA YOGA [*haṭhayoga*]
Yogic practices, both physical and mental, performed for the purpose of purifying and strengthening the physical and subtle bodies. *See also* YOGA.

INTENSIVE
A Siddha Yoga meditation program designed by Swami Muktananda to give direct initiation through the awakening of the *kundalinī* energy. *See also* KUNDALINI; SHAKTIPAT.

KARMA [*karma*]
(*lit.*, action) 1) Any action — physical, verbal, or mental. 2) Destiny, which is caused by past actions, mainly those of previous lives.

KASHI
The ancient name for the North Indian city of Varanasi, or Benares, sacred to Lord Shiva. According to Hindu tradition, whoever dies in Kashi attains liberation.

KASHMIR SHAIVISM
A branch of the Shaivite philosophical tradition, propounded by Kashmiri sages, that explains how the formless supreme Principle, Shiva, manifests as the universe.

KHECHARI MUDRA [*khecarīmudrā*]
An advanced yogic technique in which the tip of the tongue curls back into the throat and upward into the nasal pharynx. This *mudrā* (gesture) breaks the *rudra granthi* (knot of Rudra) in the *sushumnā nāḍī*, permitting the *kundalinī* to rise to the *sahasrāra*, and causing the meditator to experience *samādhi* states and taste divine nectar.

KOMALA [*komala*]
Tender; soft.

KRISHNA [*kṛṣṇa*]
(*lit.*, the dark one) The eighth incarnation of Lord Vishnu. The spiritual teachings of Lord Krishna, called "the dark one" because his skin was blue, are contained in the *Bhagavad Gītā*, a portion of the epic *Mahābhārata*. *See also* VISHNU.

KULARNAVA TANTRA
[*kulārṇavatantra*]
A Shaiva treatise about the Guru, the disciple, the mantra, and many traditional practices of worship.

KUNDALINI [*kuṇḍalinī*]
(*lit.*, coiled one) The supreme power, primordial *shakti*, or energy, that lies coiled at the base of the spine in the *mūlādhāra chakra* of every human being. Through the descent of grace (*shaktipāt*), this extremely subtle force, also described as the supreme Goddess, is awakened and begins to purify the entire being. As Kundalini travels upward through the central channel (*sushumnā nāḍī*), She pierces the various subtle energy centers (chakras) until She finally reaches the *sahasrāra* at the crown of the head. There, the individual self merges into the supreme Self, and the cycle of birth and death comes to an end. *See also* CHAKRA; SHAKTIPAT.

LAKSHMI [*lakṣmī*]
An aspect of the divine Mother; the beautiful goddess of prosperity and abundance. Portrayed as the beloved of Lord Vishnu, the sustainer of the universe, she is the source of material and spiritual blessings and all auspiciousness.

MAHABHARATA [*mahābhārata*]
An epic poem that recounts the struggle between the Kauravas and Pandavas over the disputed kingdom of Bharata, the ancient name for India. Within this vast narrative is contained a wealth of Indian secular and religious lore. The *Bhagavad Gītā* occurs in the latter portion of the *Mahābhārata*.

MAHAPRASAD [*mahāprasāda*]
(*lit.*, great blessed gift) A great blessing bestowed by the Guru or God.

MAHARASHTRA
A state on the west coast of central India, where Gurudev Siddha Peeth, the mother ashram of Siddha Yoga, is located. Many poet-saints of India lived in Maharashtra.

MANTHARA [*mantharā*]
In the *Rāmāyana*, childhood nurse of Kaikeyi, who was the second wife of Rama's father. Out of jealousy, Manthara urged Kaikeyi to demand that Rama's father send him into exile.

MANTRA [*mantra*]
(*lit.*, sacred invocation) The names of God; sacred words or divine sounds invested with the power to protect, purify, and transform the individual who repeats them. *See also* OM NAMAH SHIVAYA; SO'HAM.

MARDAVAM [*mardavam*]
Gentleness.

MAYA [*māyā*]
(*lit.*, to measure) The term used in Vedanta for the power that veils the true nature of the Self and projects the experiences of multiplicity and separation from God.

MRIDU [*mṛdu*]
Soft; delicate, pliant.

MULADHARA CHAKRA
[*mūlādhāracakra*]
The first chakra, or lowest of the seven major energy centers in the subtle body, situated at the base of the spine, where consciousness is mainly concerned with survival. Here the *kundalinī* lies coiled three-and-a-half times, dormant until awakened by grace. *See also* CHAKRA; KUNDALINI; SHAKTIPAT.

NATARAJ [*nāṭarāja*]
(*lit.*, king of the dance) A name of Shiva, referring to the dancing Shiva. The object of His dance is to free all souls from the fetters of illusion.

NIRANTARA [*nirantara*]
(*lit.*, without a gap) Continuous, uninterrupted, eternal; flowing like a stream.

OM NAMAH SHIVAYA
[*oṃ namaḥ śivāya*]
(*lit.*, *Om*, salutations to Shiva) The Sanskrit mantra of the Siddha Yoga lineage; known as the great redeeming mantra because of its power to grant both worldly fulfillment and spiritual realization. *Om* is the primordial sound; *shivāya* denotes divine Consciousness, the Lord who dwells in every heart; *namah* is to honor or to bow to.

PANDHARPUR
A place of pilgrimage in Maharashtra state, and the center of worship for devotees of Vitthal, a form of Lord Krishna. *See also* VITTHAL.

PARAMAHAMSA [*paramahaṃsa*]
One who has completely mastered all of his senses; one who has attained Self-realization.

PRANA [*prāṇa*]
The vital life-sustaining force of both the individual and the entire universe.

PRANAM [*praṇāma*]
To bow; to greet with respect.

PUJA [*pūjā*]
1) The performance of worship. 2) An altar with images of the Guru or deity and objects used in worship.

PURNO'HAM VIMARSHA
[*pūrṇo 'haṃ vimarśa*]
(*lit.*, perfect I-consciousness) The state in which one experiences identification with supreme Consciousness.

RAMA [*rāma*]
(*lit.*, one who is pleasing, delightful) The seventh incarnation of Lord Vishnu, Rama is seen as the embodiment of dharma and is the object of great devotion. He is the central character in the Indian epic *Rāmāyana. See also* RAMAYANA.

RAMAYANA [*rāmāyaṇa*]
Attributed to the sage Valmiki and one of the great epic poems of India, the *Rāmāyana* recounts the life and exploits of Lord Rama, the seventh incarnation of Vishnu. *See also* VISHNU.

RASA [*rasa*]
1) Flavor, taste. 2) A subtle energy of richness, sweetness, and delight.

RIG VEDA [*ṛgveda*]
The oldest of the four Vedas, the *Rig Veda* is composed of more than a thousand hymns, including those that invite the gods to the fire rituals. *See also* VEDAS.

RUDRA [*rudra*]
A name of Lord Shiva meaning "Lord of Tears." A figure of supreme radiance, Rudra has been revered since Vedic times as the source of all: creator, sustainer, and destroyer. As the fierce aspect of God, Rudra inspires both great love

and great fear among his worshipers. *See also* SHIVA.

RUDRA GRANTHI *See* GRANTHI.

RUDRAKSHA [*rudrākṣa*]
Seeds from a tree sacred to Shiva often strung as beads for rosaries (*mālās*). Legend has it that the *rudrāksha* seed was created from the tears of Lord Rudra; thus it is endowed with spiritual power.

SADA [*sadā*]
(*lit.*, always) Continually; perpetually.

SADGURU [*sadguru*]
A true Guru; divine Master.

SADGURUNATH MAHARAJ KI JAY!
A Hindi phrase that means "I hail the Master who has revealed the Truth to me!" An exalted, joyful expression of gratitude to the Guru for all that has been received, often repeated at the beginning or end of an action.

SADHANA [*sādhanā*]
1) A spiritual discipline or path. 2) Practices, both physical and mental, on the spiritual path.

SAHASRARA [*sahasrāra*]
The thousand-petaled spiritual energy center at the crown of the head, where one experiences the highest states of consciousness. *See also* CHAKRA; KUNDALINI.

SAKSHAT [*sākṣāt*]
Manifest; evident.

SAMADHI [*samādhi*]
The state of meditative union with the Absolute.

SAMSKARA(S) [*saṃskāra*]
Impressions of past actions and thoughts that remain in the subtle body. They are brought to the surface of one's awareness and then eliminated by the action of the awakened *kundalinī* energy. See also KARMA.

SANTOSHA [*santoṣa*]
Satisfaction; contentedness.

SARASWATI [*sarasvatī*]
(*lit.*, the flowing one) An aspect of the divine Mother; the Shakti, or creative power of the Lord; the goddess of speech, learning, and the arts.

SARVADA [*sarvadā*]
Constantly; always.

SATSANG [*satsaṅga*]
(*lit.*, the company of the Truth) The company of saints and devotees; a gathering of devotees for the purpose of chanting, meditation, and listening to scriptural teachings or readings.

SATSVARUPA [*satsvarūpa*]
One's own true form.

SATYA YUGA [*satyayuga*]
The "Golden Age," one of the four classical ages according to the Puranas. During Satya Yuga, lives are long and people heroic. Dharma, the performance of duty, is spontaneous; purity, compassion, and truthfulness abound.

SAUMYA [*saumya*]
Placid; gentle; mild.

SEVA [*sevā*]
(*lit.*, service) Selfless service; work offered to God, performed without attachment and with the attitude that one is not the doer. In Siddha Yoga ashrams, *gurusevā* is a spiritual practice, and students seek to perform all of their tasks — washing dishes, sweeping walkways, teaching courses — in this spirit of selfless offering.

SHAKTI [*śakti*]
1) The divine Mother, the dynamic aspect of supreme Shiva and the creative force of the universe. 2) The spiritual energy, *shakti. See also* KUNDALINI.

SHAKTIPAT [*śaktipāta*]
(*lit.*, descent of grace) Yogic initiation

in which the Siddha Guru transmits his spiritual energy into the aspirant, thereby awakening the aspirant's dormant *kuṇḍalinī*. *See also* GURU; KUNDALINI.

**SHAKUNI** [*śakuni*]
The notoriously wicked uncle of Duryodhana in the epic *Mahābhārata*, who worked to drive the Pandavas out of the kingdom and whose evil actions led to the great eighteen-day war.

**SHIVA** [*śiva*]
1) A name for the one supreme Reality. 2) One of the Hindu trinity of gods, representing God as the destroyer, often understood by yogis as the destroyer of barriers to one's identification with the supreme Self. In his personal form, Shiva is portrayed as a yogi wearing a tiger skin and holding a trident.

**SHIVA DRISHTI** [*śivadṛṣṭi*]
(*lit.*, the outlook of Shiva) The state of equipoise and equality-consciousness.

**SHIVA MANASA PUJA**
[*śiva-mānasa-pūjā*]
An exquisite Sanskrit hymn in which the devotee mentally worships Shiva in the form of rich and beautiful objects offered on the altar of the heart. In Siddha Yoga meditation ashrams, this text typically follows the chanting of the *Shiva Mahimnah Stotram*.

**SHIVA SAMHITA** [*śiva-saṃhitā*]
A Sanskrit text on yoga in which Ishwara, the Lord, describes the correspondence of the universe to the human body, explaining how the practices of hatha yoga and mantra yoga may be used to awaken the inner spiritual power. *See also* KUNDALINI.

**SHREE MUKTANANDA ASHRAM**
The Siddha Yoga meditation ashram in South Fallsburg, New York, established in 1979 as the international headquarters of SYDA Foundation, the nonprofit organization that administers Siddha Yoga courses and publications.

**SHRI** [*śrī*]
1) Diffusing light or radiance. 2) Sacredness; abundance; beauty; grace; auspiciousness.

**SHRIMAD BHAGAVATAM**
[*śrīmadbhāgavatam*]
One of the Puranas consisting of ancient legends of the various incarnations of the Lord; includes the life and exploits of Lord Krishna and stories of the sages and their disciples; also known as the *Bhāgavata Purāṇa*.

**SIDDHA** [*siddha*]
A perfected yogi; one who lives in the state of unity-consciousness; one whose experience of the supreme Self is uninterrupted and whose identification with the ego has been dissolved.

**SIDDHA YOGA** [*siddhayoga*]
(*lit.*, the yoga of perfection) A path to union of the individual and the Divine that begins with *shaktipāt*, the inner awakening by the grace of a Siddha Guru. Siddha Yoga is the name Swami Muktananda gave to this path, which he first brought to the West in 1970; Swami Chidvilasananda is its living Master. *See also* GURU; KUNDALINI; SHAKTIPAT.

**SIDDHA YOGA MEDITATION CENTER**
A place where people gather to practice Siddha Yoga meditation. There are over six hundred Siddha Yoga centers around the world.

**SITA** [*sītā*]
(*lit.*, the daughter of the earth) An embodiment of Lakshmi and the beloved of Lord Rama, the seventh incarnation of Lord Vishnu. Her story is told in the epic *Rāmāyana*.

**SO'HAM** [*so 'ham*]
(*lit.*, I am That) *So'ham* is the mantra that expresses the natural vibration of

the Self, which occurs spontaneously with each incoming and outgoing breath. By becoming aware of *So'ham*, a seeker experiences the identity between the individual self and the supreme Self.

**SPANDA** [*spanda*]
The vibration of divine Consciousness that pervades all life and is perceived by the yogi in higher states of meditation.

**SUFI**
One who practices Sufism, the mystical path of love in the Islamic tradition.

**SUPREME PRINCIPLE**
*See* ABSOLUTE.

**SUSHUMNA NADI** [*suṣumnānāḍī*]
The central and most important of all the seventy-two million subtle nerve channels in the human body, the *sushumnā* extends from the *mūlādhāra chakra* at the base of the spine to the *sahasrāra* at the top of the head, and contains all the other major chakras. *See also* CHAKRA; KUNDALINI.

**SWADHYAYA** [*svādhyāya*]
The study of the Self; the practice of reciting spiritual texts, often in song.

**TANTRALOKA** [*tantrāloka*]
A massive and encyclopedic work by Abhinavagupta in twelve volumes, containing the Shaiva philosophy and practices in all their aspects. *See also* KASHMIR SHAIVISM.

**TAO TE CHING**
(*lit.*, the way and its virtue) The classic scripture of Taoism by the Chinese sage Lao-tsu, which holds that there is a basic principle of harmony in the universe, known as the Tao.

**TAPASYA** [*tapasya*]
1) Austerities. 2) The fire of yoga; the experience of heat generated by spiritual practices.

**TEMPLE, THE**
Unless it is otherwise specified, "the Temple" refers to the Bhagawan Nityananda Temple in Shree Muktananda Ashram or in Gurudev Siddha Peeth.

**TURIYA** [*turīya*]
The fourth or transcendental state, beyond the waking, dream, and deep-sleep states, in which the true nature of reality is directly perceived; the state of *samādhi*, or deep meditation.

**UPANISHADS** [*upaniṣad*]
(*lit.*, sitting close to; secret teachings) The inspired teachings, visions, and mystical experiences of the ancient sages of India. With immense variety of form and style, all of these scriptures (exceeding one hundred texts) give the same essential teaching: that the individual soul and God are one. *See also* VEDAS; VEDANTA.

**VAIKUNTHA** [*vaikuṇṭha*]
The abode of Lord Vishnu; heaven.

**VEDANTA** [*vedānta*]
(*lit.*, end of the Vedas) One of the six orthodox schools of Indian philosophy; usually identified as Advaita ("nondual") Vedanta, meaning that there is one supreme Principle that is the foundation of the universe. *See also* VEDAS.

**VEDAS** [*veda*]
(*lit.*, knowledge) Among the most ancient, revered, and sacred of the world's scriptures, the four Vedas are regarded as divinely revealed, eternal wisdom. They are the *Rig Veda, Atharva Veda, Sāma Veda*, and *Yajur Veda*. *See also* ATHARVA VEDA; RIG VEDA.

**VIJNANA BHAIRAVA**
[*vijñānabhairava*]
An exposition of the path of yoga based on the principles of Kashmir Shaivism. Originally revealed in Sanskrit, probably in the seventh century, it is a compilation of 112 *dhāranās*, centering tech-

niques, any of which can give the immediate experience of union with God.

VIMATSARA [*vimatsara*]
Free from envy or jealousy.

VISHNU [*viṣṇu*]
1) The all-pervasive supreme Reality. 2) One of the Hindu trinity of gods, representing God as the sustainer of the universe. Rama and Krishna are the best known of his incarnations.

VISHNU GRANTHI *See* GRANTHI.

VISHNU SAHASRANAMA
[*viṣṇusahasranāma*]
(*lit.*, the thousand names of Vishnu)
A hymn honoring Vishnu, regularly chanted in Siddha Yoga meditation ashrams.

VITTHAL [*viṭṭhaḷa*]
A form of Krishna whose image is enshrined in Pandharpur, a famous place of pilgrimage in Maharashtra. Vitthal was eulogized by the poet-saints of Maharashtra and Karnataka.

YOGA [*yoga*]
(*lit.*, union) The spiritual practices and disciplines that lead a seeker to evenness of mind, to the severing of the union with pain, and, through detachment, to skill in action. Ultimately, the path of yoga leads to the constant experience of the Self.

YOGA SUTRAS [*yoga-sūtra*]
A collection of aphorisms, attributed to the fourth-century sage Patanjali. This is the basic scripture of *ashtānga yoga*, the "eight-limbed path" to Self-realization that takes a seeker through specific stages to the state of total absorption in God.

YOGI [*yogī*]
1) One who practices yoga. 2) One who has attained perfection through yogic practices.

YUDHISHTHIRA [*yudhiṣṭhira*]
The eldest of the five Pandava brothers, heroes in the *Mahābhārata*, and the son of Dharma.

# Index

# *Further Reading*

*Play of Consciousness* — SWAMI MUKTANANDA

In this intimate and powerful portrait, Swami Muktananda describes his own journey to Self-realization, revealing the process of transformation he experienced under the guidance of his Guru, Bhagawan Nityananda.

*From the Finite to the Infinite* — SWAMI MUKTANANDA

This compilation of questions and answers is drawn from Baba Muktananda's travels in the West. In it, Baba addresses all the issues a seeker might encounter on the spiritual path, from the earliest days until the culmination of the journey.

*Where Are You Going?* — SWAMI MUKTANANDA

A comprehensive introduction to the teachings of Siddha Yoga meditation, this lively and anecdotal book explores the nature of the mind, the Self, the inner power, as well as mantra, meditation, and the Guru.

*I Have Become Alive* — SWAMI MUKTANANDA

Here Baba Muktananda shows us how to integrate the inner quest with the demands of contemporary life. He illumines such topics as spiritual discipline, the ego, marriage, parenting, experiencing love, and attaining God while embracing the world.

*Bhagawan Nityananda of Ganeshpuri* — SWAMI MUKTANANDA

He rarely spoke, but a brief sentence from him spoke volumes, guiding the fortunate listener across the sea of illusion. This volume on the life of Bhagawan Nityananda is filled with the observations, thoughts, and offerings of praise — compiled from many sources, over many years — by his successor, the Siddha Master Swami Muktananda.

*Secret of the Siddhas* — SWAMI MUKTANANDA

For thousands of years, the teachings of the Siddha Masters have been handed down from Guru to disciple. Here Swami Muktananda introduces us to the extraordinary lineage of Siddhas and interprets some basic tenets of Vedanta and Kashmir Shaivism, two philsophical schools at the heart of Siddha Yoga.

*Kundalini: The Secret of Life* — SWAMI MUKTANANDA

The awakening of *kundalinī*, the latent spiritual energy within us, marks the beginning of our journey to perfection. But what is the nature of this mighty force of transformation? How is it awakened? And how can its progress be nurtured? Swami Muktananda addresses this topic, which is so vital to every spiritual seeker.

***The Yoga of Discipline*** SWAMI CHIDVILASANANDA

"From the standpoint of the spiritual path," Swami Chidvilasananda says, "the term *discipline* is alive with the joyful expectancy of divine fulfillment." In this series of talks on practicing and cultivating discipline of the senses, Gurumayi shows us how this practice brings great joy.

***My Lord Loves a Pure Heart: The Yoga of Divine Virtues***
SWAMI CHIDVILASANANDA

Fearlessness, reverence, compassion, freedom from anger — Gurumayi describes how these magnificent virtues are an integral part of our true nature. The list of virtues introduced in this volume is based on Chapter Sixteen of the *Bhagavad Gītā.*

***Inner Treasures*** SWAMI CHIDVILASANANDA

"Every heart blazes with divine light," Gurumayi says. "Every heart trembles with divine love." In these inspiring talks, she offers us practical ways to cultivate the inner treasures: peace, joy, and love.

***Kindle My Heart*** SWAMI CHIDVILASANANDA

The first of Gurumayi Chidvilasananda's books, this is an introduction to the classic themes of the spiritual journey, arranged thematically. There are chapters on such subjects as meditation, mantra, control of the senses, the Guru, the disciple, and the state of a great being.

## *Books of Contemplations*

***The Magic of the Heart: Reflections on Divine Love***
SWAMI CHIDVILASANANDA

In these profound and tender reflections on divine love, Gurumayi Chidvilasananda makes it clear that the supreme Heart is a place we must get to know. It is here, she tells us, in the interior of the soul, that "the Lord reveals Himself every second of the day."

***Resonate with Stillnesss: Daily Contemplations***
SWAMI CHIDVILASANANDA *and* SWAMI MUKTANANDA

Every sentence of this exquisite collection of contemplations is an expression of wisdom and love from the Siddha Masters Baba Muktananda and Gurumayi Chidvilasananda. The selections are dated and arranged in twelve themes of spiritual life, with a contemplation for each day of the year.

### *Be Filled with Enthusiasm and Sing God's Glory*

The contemplations in this pocket-sized book can help us to imbibe Gurumayi's message wherever we are throughout the day. Our own enthusiasm is ignited by these quotes of Gurumayi, of Baba Muktananda, and of saints and sages from many traditions around the world.

## *Books of Poetry*

### *Mukteshwari* — SWAMI MUKTANANDA

Baba Muktananda guides us through the stages of the spiritual path, inviting us to throw off our limitations and join him in the state of total freedom. These autobiographical verses, among Baba's earliest writings, are now offered in this new, single-volume edition, featuring nine photos of Baba.

### *Ashes at My Guru's Feet* — SWAMI CHIDVILASANANDA

In this priceless collection of her poetry, offered to her Guru, Swami Muktananda, Gurumayi generously shares with us her own experience of the spiritual path. In the universal language of poetry, Gurumayi portrays how the path of love for the Guru can burn the ego to ashes and open the disciple to purest light. *Illustrated.*

You may learn more about the teachings and
practices of Siddha Yoga Meditation by contacting:

SYDA Foundation
371 Brickman Rd.
P.O. Box 600
South Fallsburg, NY 12779-0600, USA
Tel: (914) 434-2000

*or*

Gurudev Siddha Peeth
P.O. Ganeshpuri
PIN 401 206
District Thana
Maharashtra, India

For further information about books in print by Swami Muktananda
and Swami Chidvilasananda, and editions in translation, please contact:

Siddha Yoga Meditation Bookstore
371 Brickman Rd.
P.O. Box 600
South Fallsburg, NY 12779-0600, USA
Tel: (914) 434-2000 ext. 1700